MY GRAMMA'S FORGOTTEN RECIPES

A Russian Jewish Holiday Cookbook

Irina in the kitchen.

IRINA TSEGER
WITH STEPHANIE SCHARF

ISBN: 978-1-60414-825-1

ACKNOWLEDGEMENTS

The authors thank Alex Tseger for contributing time and effort to producing all of the photographs in this book, for which we are very grateful.

We also thank Lena Fridman and Sandra Leavitt for their editorial contributions.

Irina and Stephanie thank their families for their support, love and encouraging the writing of this book.

CONTENTS

YOM KIPPUR

SUCCOT

CHANUKAH

PASSOVER

INTRODUCTION

For too many years, traditional Jewish holiday foods were contained in packages and jars. Today's adults with Russian Jewish roots are unlikely to have heard Yiddish or Russian spoken at home, tasted homemade gefilte fish, and probably think that the Catskills is an animal training book. Most American Jews are descendants of the great waves of Russian Jewish emigration in the late 19th and early 20th centuries, which brought some 2 million Eastern European Jews to this country. Many had roots in Russia, Ukraine and Poland.

Almost as soon as they immigrated to the United States, these hardy Russian Jews began the process of assimilation. While foreign language and social skills, along with early 20th century American prejudice, limited their entry into American society, the immigrants set their sights on the next generation, preparing their children to move in broader American economic and social circles. At the same time their children and grandchildren moved toward assimilation, their parents' homes typically maintained the same style and cuisine found in their original Russian roots.

Over time, and with the popularity of Reform Judaism, along with the geographic and temporal distance from Russian Jewish life, most Russian Jews lost their roots. Many forsook old country practices in their desire to become accepted as

full Americans. While Jewish holiday gatherings took place in Gramma's house, after her generation passed on, many families dispersed to different locations in the country and their gatherings became a distant memory.

In the last part of the 20th century, Americans of Russian Jewish ancestry began to support a second wave of Russian Jewish immigration as pre-*glasnost, glasnost* and *perestroika* permitted Russian Jews to emigrate. The modern wave of Russian Jewish immigrants provided the opportunity to reconnect with traditional customs and cuisine maintained by those who remained in Russia. This cookbook stems from the life of one such immigrant, Irina Tseger.

Like virtually all Jews living in 20th century Russia, Irina experienced a very different Jewish life than those of us living in America. She was born immediately after World War II and immigrated to America from Russia in 1990. She was raised in Dnepropetrovsk, a large city south of Kiev, Ukraine. She was raised in a two-room apartment with her mother, two sisters and Gramma Eda. They shared a toilet and kitchen with another family, boiling water inside the apartment in order to bathe. There was no telephone.

Post-WW II Russian Jews were subject to persecution. Russian Jews could not practice their religion publicly. To advance required becoming

Russianized. Irina recalls that her cousin had straight A's in high school studying advanced math but she couldn't advance to university because her parents were Jewish. She changed her last name, retook the entrance exam, and then was allowed to attend university.

This story is not unique as large numbers of Jews had to abandon any outward appearance of being Jewish due to fear of the social and economic consequences. Yet many Russian Jews upheld the culture in the privacy of their homes. And that culture included a rich array of the foods that are identified throughout the Western world with Jewish culture and holidays.

In Irina's house, Gramma was in charge of the family meals, with a style of cooking born in equal parts from scarcity and creativity, much as earlier generations of Russian Jews cooked. This was not a culture in which you planned meals and bought the ingredients you needed. Rather, shopping was daily, and because one could never be sure of what would be available, meals were devised from what one could grow or buy. Every day, Gramma sent Irina to buy groceries. She stood in separate lines for meat, milk and vegetables. Sometimes she would find staples at the farmers' market. Gramma then created her own recipes, making do with what was available that day.

The family never threw food in the garbage; every bit of leftovers including a scrap of bread, was used for another meal. Gramma would put old fruit and cinnamon on the bread, bake it, and out came a cake. There were no utensils beyond the basics. Gramma mixed everything by hand, which took hours and was very difficult.

Jewish holidays were celebrated in secret. Jews didn't talk about Jewish holidays or go to religious school. Irina's family had Shabbat at home but Irina didn't understand that their Friday night rituals were Jewish until she was close to adulthood. Every Friday Gramma went to the farmers' market and made chicken soup and fish for dinner.

Grandfather went to the Turkish bath, and then to synagogue in a small shack under a bridge that had no outward sign of Judaism. This was how Jews found a place to get together, in one shack in a city of over one million. As Friday approached, Gramma would close the windows with wooden shutters so no one would see that she was serving traditional Jewish foods.

Passover, like Shabbat, was celebrated in secrecy at home. Each year around Passover, Irina's uncles secretly sent matzo from Moscow. Gramma also used to bake her own, at night when the neighbors were asleep.

Gramma kept a locked wooden box covered with a cloth, which doubled as a kitchen table. When Irina was a child she never knew what was inside and Gramma never opened the box in front of her. Once, just before Passover, Gramma asked Irina to help her remove dishes from this box. When it was opened, Irina saw a talit and books which revealed to her that the family was Jewish and that the religion had to be kept hidden. When Irina was older, Grampa would wear the talit at home on Fridays and Jewish holidays but Gramma cautioned Irina not to tell anyone.

In spite of these barriers, Gramma was proud to be Jewish. She used to say: "Look how we Jewish people make do. You should be proud that we are Jewish." When Irina came to the United States it was the first time she could tell anyone outside of her family that she was Jewish. She began to celebrate her religious freedom and the Jewish holidays with Russian Jewish cooking.

Today, Irina recalls the past and looks forward to a different future:

"I am dedicating this book to my grandmother Eda, whom I resemble, and my mom, Luba, who inspired me to come to America. Gramma always

cooked from what was available at home, creating her own recipes, and amazed everyone around her. I helped her in the kitchen and developed a love for the culinary arts. In America there are many opportunities to achieve one's aspirations and for that reason I have chosen to accomplish mine through this cookbook. It is my hope that this book will help families to grow closer by bringing parents, children, family and friends into the kitchen together.

Putting love into your cooking makes it appetizing and so much better tasting! Much good luck to you in the kitchen preparing for a good Yontov with your family beside you as you cook."

ABOUT THE RECIPES IN THIS BOOK

Our recipes highlight cooking traditions from the five holidays that are most commonly observed by Jews in the 21st century: Rosh Hashanah, Yom Kippur, Succot, Chanukah, and Passover. Because many recipes are not as well known today as a generation ago, we have used photographs liberally to illustrate the various phases of complicated dishes. Each recipe has been kitchen-tested by Americans who had never before prepared that dish to ensure that the recipe was useful to even the most inexperienced cook.

In Russia, certain foods were not readily available and the recipes and their ingredients reflect these differences. Butter, for example, was expensive and often was substituted with vegetable oil or olive oil. Beets, carrots, radishes, green onions, tomatoes, cucumbers and potatoes were commonly used vegetables. Especially in winter, carrots, cabbage and apples were used. Eggs were the most common source of protein although beef and chicken were also available. Carp was a common fish purchased at the farmers' market. Salmon, on the other hand, was extremely expensive. Baking was a common method of cooking, and Irina remembers her childhood home filled with the smell of vanilla and cinnamon.

We have categorized recipes within Jewish holidays although many of the dishes can be used interchangeably for any festive meal. A few dishes are associated with a specific holiday (e.g., latkes for Chanukah), but today most are served at different times of the year (e.g., gefilte fish for Rosh Hashanah and Passover). We encourage you to leaf through the entire book to pick and choose what you would like to cook at any time of the year.

NOTE ON COOKING UTENSILS

The recipes are written to use utensils commonly found in American kitchens. In Russia, there were no modern conveniences such as electric food processors or grinders. For our recipes, the most frequently used cooking utensils include:

- Grater/shredder (for cheese and vegetables)— a 4-sided hand grater/shredder because each side provides a different level of fineness

- Good knife for cutting vegetables

- Glass or stainless steel mixing bowls of different sizes

- Food processor (instead of a hand grinder, which is what Russians used)

- Electric mixer, either a tabletop or hand-held model (instead of whipping by hand)

- 10-inch pan

- 5-quart and 8-quart cooking pots

- Hand chopper

NOTE ON INGREDIENTS

- When milk is called for, you can use 2 percent milk or whole milk (but not skim milk).

- When sour cream is called for, you can use low-fat sour cream or Greek yoghurt.

ROSH HASHANAH

Turnip and mushroom salad.

SALADS

TURNIP AND MUSHROOM SALAD

Ingredients:

2 medium or 1 large onion

2 turnips, shredded in large-hole shredder

5 medium or 2 large Portobello mushrooms

Fresh dill (a few sprigs)

Rinse turnips, peel with a carrot scraper, and shred.

Slice mushrooms in thin slices.

Cut onion in half, and thinly slice each half.

Stir-fry the onions and mushrooms. When onions are golden, remove from pan and mix with turnips. Salt and pepper to taste. Sprinkle with chopped dill leaves.

Refrigerate and serve chilled.

Serves 4

RADISH SALAD

Ingredients:

4 bunches radishes

2 cups sour cream

2 bunches green onions

2 tablespoons fresh chopped dill

8 hard-boiled eggs

Slice radishes into thin slices. Chop the green onions, including the white part. Cut the eggs into very small cubes. Combine all ingredients. Serve cold.

To serve: layer the bottom of a serving plate with purple lettuce leave around the edge of the plate, for a ruffled effect. Spoon salad in middle of plate and on top of ends of leaves.

Serves 12

CABBAGE SALAD

Ingredients:

1 green cabbage

1/2 bunch green onions

1/4 red cabbage

1/2 cup pine nuts

2 small cucumbers

1/2 cup dried cranberries or dried blueberries

2 tbsp olive oil

Slice cabbages into very thin slices. Cut the cucumbers lengthwise in half and then cut thin slices of half moons. Chop the green onions. Mix all ingredients together. Place in serving bowl.

Serves 12

CARROT AND TOMATO SALAD

Ingredients:

10 fresh carrots

10-15 cherry tomatoes

10 cloves of freshly chopped garlic

2 sprigs parsley

6 tablespoons mayonnaise

1 head of leafy lettuce

Directions:

Using a shredder shred the carrots into long, thin pieces (using medium sized shredding holes). Squeeze garlic in a garlic press. Mix carrots, the squeezed garlic and mayonnaise.

To serve: Place lettuce leaves around outside of plate to mimic the effect of a ruffled hem around the plate. Spoon the mixture onto the middle of the plate, covering the inside ends of the lettuce leaves. Cut cherry tomatoes in half and place them around the edge of the plate as a border for the salad, flat side facing out. Place a small sprig of parsley in between each tomato slice.

Serves 12

BEET SALAD

Ingredients:

3 fresh beets

1 cup whole walnuts

4 cloves fresh garlic (optional)

2-4 tablespoons of mayonnaise

1 cup pitted prunes (or dried cherries/cranberries)

(Optional: substitute sour cream or Greek yoghurt)

Directions:

Remove stems of beets, wash beets but do not skin. Place beets in a pot well covered with water. Boil the water. After water comes to a boil, turn down heat to a simmer and cook for about 40 minutes to an hour until a toothpick goes smoothly into the beets.

Drain water and place beets immediately in cold water for a couple of minutes until they are cool enough to work with. Peel the beets. Shred with the large hole shredder. Add walnuts, pitted prunes (or dried cherries or dried cranberries), and squeezed garlic (optional). Add mayonnaise to taste (start with 2 tablespoons) and mix. Add salt and pepper to taste.

To serve: Chill and place salad on a bed of lettuce or with other vegetable garnish. **Serves 6**.

Beet salad garnished with prunes and walnuts.

SOUPS

CHICKEN SOUP WITH VERINIKIES (DUMPLINGS)

Ingredients:

1 whole chicken

2 yellow onions

1 large carrot

1 bunch of parsley

1 bunch of dill (optional)

2 yolks

1 cup flour

salt

1/4 cup boiled water

olive oil (enough for frying onion)

1 lemon

Note: For directions for making verinikies (dumplings) see next page.

Rinse the chicken pieces. Place in a pot and add enough cold water to just cover the chicken. Bring to a boil and cook for 1 minute. Drain the water and rinse the chicken well.

Fill most of a large pot with clear water and bring to a boil. Then place the chicken in and return it to a boil. The amount of water in the pot should cover the chicken 3 times over. Add the onion and large carrot. Once the water is again boiling, lower the heat to a very slow simmer. In 45 minutes, add the parsley, baby carrots and garlic. Salt to taste (at least 1/4 tsp). Cook for 5 minutes. Turn off heat and keep covered for another 30 minutes. Use a slotted spoon to remove all the vegetables except the baby carrots.

To serve: Ladle individual portions of soup. Place 3 dumplings in each bowl, adding one slice of carrot from the cooked soup, a sprig of fresh parsley, and a small thin slice of lemon. Optional: Add a piece of chicken and sprinkle a little parsley on top. Or, you can serve the chicken separately as part of a main course.

VERINIKIES

To make the filling: grind the cooked chicken. Determine what type of food processor slicer to use, or use a hand grinder. Chop 1 fresh onion into cubes and fry it in two tbsp olive oil along with salt and pepper to taste. Mix cooked onion, chicken and raw egg. Add 1 tbsp of chopped parsley or chopped dill, whichever you prefer. Cover the mixture and put it into the refrigerator.

To make the dough: put flour in a mixing bowl and add the boiled water. Mix well and then add the two egg yolks. Mix in the yolks. Pick up a ball of dough — it should not stick to your hand. If it does, add in some additional flour (a teaspoon at a time) until the dough does not stick to your hand. Put the ball of dough on a cutting board.

To make the verinikies: roll dough flat. Use a glass or measuring cup with a 2-inch diameter to cut out pieces of dough. In the middle of each dough round, put a spoonful of stuffing and fold the dough over to make a half-moon shaped dumpling. Place formed dumplings on a flat plan or flat glass/plastic plate, so they are separate, and place in freezer for 20 minutes. Remove from freezer and place the dumplings in boiling water for 1 minute. Remove from water with a slotted spoon, and put into soup. Makes about 45 pieces of verinikies.

Note: Dumplings can be made in advance. Once completed, place in freezer for 20 minutes so they are sufficiently chilled and do not stick together. Then, place dumplings in a plastic freezer bag until they are ready to cook, as above, in boiling water. They do not need to be defrosted to cook.

COLD BEET BORSCHT

Ingredients to cook the soup:

2 large red beets

2 large lemons

12 cups water

2 medium red potatoes (peeled and cut into 1-inch cubes)

1 large soup pot

Ingredients to serve the soup:

1 bunch scallions, rinsed and chopped

1 lemon, cut into thin slices

1 bunch parsley, rinsed and chopped

3 medium cucumbers, peeled and cubed

6 eggs, hard boiled

Greek yoghurt or sour cream

Directions:

Rinse the beets well. Put beets together with 12 cups of water in a large soup pot. Cover and bring to a boil. Once the water boils, lower flame so that the soup simmers for 30 minutes. Take the beets out of the water, place into a bowl and put under cold running water until the beets are cool.

Place the peeled onion and the cubed potatoes into the beet water with a low flame so that the soup continues to simmer. Cook for 15 minutes. In the meantime, peel and shred the cooked beets in the large-hole shredder. Add the shredded beets to the simmering soup. Remove and discard onion.

Turn off flame and add juice of two lemons. Sprinkle salt into soup. Add parsley to the soup. Mix ingredients. Once the soup cools down, put the soup into the refrigerator to chill. It will probably take 12 hours to chill until cold. You may also cook and peel the hard boiled eggs at this time and then put into refrigerator to chill.

To serve: In each individual soup dish, place these garnishes: 1/2 chopped cucumber; 1 hard-boiled egg chopped or cut into halves; chopped green onion. Once the garnishes are in the bowl, ladle the soup into the bowl. Add a teaspoon of sour cream or Greek yoghurt. Top the sour cream or yoghurt with a slice of lemon and serve.

Serves 6

Cold beet borscht.

CHICKEN SOUP

This is the classic Jewish dish, traditionally served Friday night or whenever anyone was sick. Scientists have even shown that chicken soup has natural healing qualities. Here is one of our favorite recipes with variations on how to serve.

Ingredients:

1 whole fresh chicken cut up into 8 pieces

Two branches of celery, unsliced.

1 large yellow onion (skin removed)

A few cloves of peeled garlic.

3 large carrots sliced in either 1-inch chunks or longer

2 whole bunches of fresh parsley (washed)

A small bag of baby carrots (about 20)

Directions:

Rinse the chicken pieces; place in enough cold water to just cover chicken and bring to a boil to 1 minute. Drain water rinse chicken well. Bring a second pot of clear water to a boil. Place chicken in the water and bring back to a boil. Use enough water to cover the chicken three times over.

Add onion. Add carrots. Once the water is boiling, lower heat so water is on a very slow simmer. In about 45 minutes, add 1 bunch of parsley, celery, baby carrots and garlic. Salt to taste (at least 1/4 teaspoon). Cook for five minutes. Turn off heat and keep covered for another 30 minutes. Use slotted spoon to remove all of the vegetables except the baby carrots. Soup is ready to serve.

To serve: Ladle soup in a bowl. Add a baby carrot and a leaf of parsley. Optional: sprinkle a little parsley on top and also a piece of chicken.

Serves 8

MAIN COURSES AND SIDE DISHES

GEFILTE FISH

In America, we think of cooked gefilte fish as fish balls. In Russia, gefilte fish was stuffed fish. Here we present two versions of the dish, one with the fish mix used to stuff fish "steaks" and the other made as fish balls.

Traditionally gefilte fish is made with pike mixed with either whitefish and/or buffalo fish.

You may buy pike and either one or both of the other fishes. Do not worry about the exact amount of fish that you buy, the recipe tolerates varying fish sizes. The recipes below make either 16 gefilte "steaks" or about 30 gefilte fish balls. It is okay to halve the recipes to make fewer pieces for each dish.

NOTE: This dish must be made at least 1-2 days in advance of serving.

Ingredients for both the fish steak recipe and the fish ball recipe:

- 2 eggs
- 4 large yellow onions (try to find extra skin from the onion bin)
- 4 large red beets
- 1/2 cup matzo meal (cereal oats can be substituted)
- 4 large (fat) carrots

- 1 tbsp sugar
- 12 bay leaves
- 1 tsp salt
- 1/2 tsp black pepper
- 1 whole pike/buffalo, 7-9 lbs.
- 1 whole whitefish and/or 1 whole buffalo fish, totaling about 7-10 lbs.

Note: Ask the store to bone and skin the fish and to put the heads, tails, bones and skin in a separate package to take with you.

Alternative: buy total of 2 pounds of fileted fish. You can also ask the store to slice the fish into slices about 3 inches wide. *(See picture on page 18.)*

Recipe-specific utensils:

Large metal baking pan or casserole pan that is at least 4 inches high.
Food processor or hand fish/meat grinder.

Picture of fresh sliced fish before preparation.

TO PREPARE GEFILTE FISH STEAKS

Cut out the flesh of the fish slices leaving the skin and bone intact. *(See pictures.)* Grind the flesh of the fish, in an electric grinder if you have one, or a food processor if you do not own a grinder. Grind fish to a consistency that allows it to be rolled into a ball. If you use a food processor, for each 2 cups of raw fish, pulse about 2 seconds each time.

Peel the onions and reserve the yellow skin. Chop or grind 1 onion into very fine pieces that are small enough to mix into a fish ball. Slice the other 3 onions into very thin slices. Slice the beets into very thin slices. Slice the carrots cross wise into 1/2-inch slices. Up to this point, preparation may take place up to 2 days in advance of cooking so long as the fish is properly refrigerated.

Vegetables, fish slices and ground fish should be stored in the refrigerator in separate containers.

Cutting flesh from the fish slice, leaving the skin and bony structure intact.

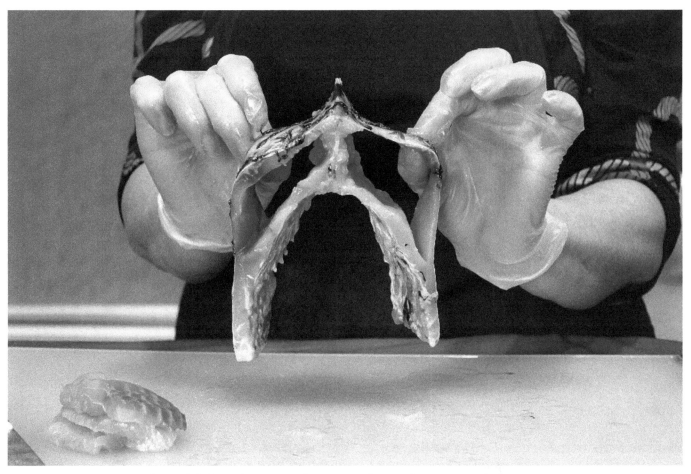

Slice of fish with meat taken out, skin and structure left intact.

To prepare for cooking:

Preheat oven to 400°F. In a bowl with the ground fish, place eggs and matzo meal together inside on one side of the bowl and mix the eggs and matzo meal together. Let sit together for a minute. Mix the ground fish, ground onion, eggs, matzo meal, salt and pepper together. Fill the cavity of each fish slice with the ground mix. *(See picture of fish slices on top of vegetables.)* If there is leftover fish, you can make balls about 2 inches in diameter and set aside for cooking. Some people like stuffed fish head, and you can also stuff the head of the fish for cooking.

Start boiling about 6 quarts of water. Line the bottom of a cooking pan with the fish bones and skin that you took home from the market, which will add flavor to the cooking fluid. (You can skip this step if you are missing these items.) Start layering the vegetables, by starting with a layer of sliced beets, cover the beet layer with a layer of sliced carrots, and then cover the carrot layer with a layer of sliced onions. *(See picture of first layer of vegetables.)*

Arrange the stuffed fish slices over the sliced onions. If you would like to cook the fish head, also place it (stuffed or unstuffed) in the pan. Place any fish balls in this fish layer as well. *(See picture of fish placed over vegetables.)* Place bay leaves down the sides of the cooking plan and put 2-3 bay leaves across top of layers. Sprinkle with black pepper to taste.

*From upper left: cut vegetables, sliced whole fish, gefilte fish mix,
and first layer of vegetables in pan.*

Layer over the fish with a layer of beets, then carrots, and then onions. Place extra carrot and beet slices into crevices of the fish and also place on top of the fish. Add additional sprinkling of salt to taste *(See picture of fish layered over with vegetables.)*

Rinse onion skins. Place a layer the onion skins over the top layer of vegetables. Caramelize sugar by heating the sugar until melted, stirring with a wooden spoon. Then add 1 cup of boiling water to the cooked sugar in the pan. Drizzle the caramelized water over the onion skins. In addition, pour enough boiling water into the pan so that the water reaches about an inch from the top of the pan. If the pan is deep enough, you can

put in enough boiling water to cover all layers of the pan including the onion skins. *(See picture of fish in pan ready for baking.)*

Place in oven uncovered. Cook for three hours. Remove from oven and let cool. Remove onion skins. Remove top layer of vegetables, discard the onions and beets, and set aside the carrots. Carefully remove balls from the fluid and place balls and carrots in a dish for refrigeration. Strain the broth of remaining fish parts and vegetables and keep strained broth for next steps.

Pour the strained fish fluid over the balls and carrots, enough to cover. Cool for at least 12 hours. If there is remaining fish broth, it can be

In preparation: gefilte fish on top of vegetables.

In preparation: gefilte fish layered over with vegetables.

Gefilte fish in pan ready for baking.

saved and then served as a plain fish broth or cooked with vegetables (like peeled potatoes) for vegetable soup.

To serve: place the fish on one main serving plate or in individual plates. Garnish with the cooked carrots and/or lemon slices. Serve with ground horseradish.

Gefilte fish "steaks" garnished with lemon and carrot slices.

TO PREPARE GEFILTE FISH BALLS (ABOUT 30 BALLS)

Grind the flesh of the fish, in an electric grinder if you have one, or a food processor if you do not own a grinder. Grind fish to a consistency that allows it to be rolled into a ball. If you use a food processor, for each 2 cups of raw fish, pulse about 2 seconds each time.

Peel the onions and reserve the yellow skin. Chop or grind 1 onion into very fine pieces that are small enough to mix into a fish ball. Slice the other 3 onions into very thin slices. Slice the beets into very thin slices. Slice the carrots crosswise into half-inch slices.

Up to this point, preparation may take place up to 2 days in advance of cooking so long as the fish is properly refrigerated. Vegetables and fish should be stored in the refrigerator in separate containers.

Directions for cooking:

Preheat oven to 400°F.

In a bowl with the ground fish, place eggs and matzo meal together inside on one side of the bowl and mix the eggs and matzo meal together. Let sit together for a minute. Mix the ground fish, ground onion, eggs, matzo meal, salt and pepper together. Use the fish mix to make balls about 2 inches in diameter. If the mixture is not tacky enough to form a ball, just add in some more matzo meal, as needed (see picture of gefilte fish balls).

Start boiling about 6 quarts of water. Line the bottom of a cooking pan with the fish bones and skin that you took home from the market, which is needed to add flavor to the cooking fluid. Start layering the vegetables, with a bottom layer of sliced beets, cover the beet layer with a layer of sliced carrots, and then cover the carrot layer with a layer of sliced onions. Gently place the fish balls on the onion layer. **Separate each fish ball with a slice of onion so that as they cook, the balls will not stick together.**

If you have enough fish mix for a second layer of balls, place sliced onions over the first layer of balls and place the second layer of balls on the sliced onions. Be careful to use an onion slice to separate the balls. Over the fish, place a layer of beets, then carrots, and then onions. Add additional sprinkling of salt to taste. Place bay leaves down the sides of the cooking plan and put 2-3 bay leaves across top of layers. Rinse the onion skins. Place a layer of the onion skins over the top layer of vegetables.

Caramelize the sugar by heating it in a small pan until melted, stirring with a wooden spoon. Then add 1 cup of boiling water to the cooked sugar. Drizzle the caramelized water over the onion skins. In addition, pour enough boiling water into the pan so that the water covers **all layers** including the onion skins.

Place in oven uncovered. Cook for 1 to 2 hours. Remove from oven and let cool. Remove onion skins. Remove top layer of carrots and other vegetables. Carefully remove fish balls. Strain and set aside the broth.

Place the fish balls and carrots in a dish for refrigeration. Pour the strained fish fluid into the dish, enough to cover the fish and carrots. (Extra broth can be saved for fish soup, eaten by itself or adding peeled potatoes and cooking until soft.) Cool at least overnight. Cooked fish may be refrigerated for up to 3 days in advance of serving.

To serve: Place the fish balls into a group serving dish or individual plates. Serve with vegetable garnishes (such as sliced carrots) and with dollops of horseradish.

Alternative presentation: Place fish balls on a platter mimicking the shape of a fish and garnish with vegetables, including vegetables for the head and tail of the fish **(see picture).**

Gefilte fish balls arranged to mimic the body of a fish with a cooked beet as the fish "head" and vegetable garnishes over the body and as a "tail."

BLINTZES

Blintzes are a typical Russian Jewish holiday meal and can be served in as many ways as your imagination allows. They can be eaten as a main course, a side dish or a dessert. They can be served warm or at room temperature after they are filled or they can be refrigerated and served cold after filling. They can be served fried or baked. However you choose to serve the dish, the basic recipe for making the blintz is the same. We start with the basic recipe for making blintzes. The basic recipe below makes about 50 blintzes.

Ingredients:

2 eggs and 1 egg yolk

4 cups milk

2 cups of flour

1 tbsp sugar

1/2 tsp vanilla powder

1 tbsp olive oil

Pinch of salt

Red or black caviar (for garnish)

Directions:

Mix eggs, yolk and salt. Add 1 cup milk and the flour, and mix by hand. The mixture will be stiff. Little by little, dribble in remaining milk. Once milk is mixed in, add the olive oil. Preheat a small 6" crepe pan. Dribble 1/2 tbsp oil into the pan and use a paper towel to spread it around. Spoon 1/4 cup of batter into the pan, and swirl it around so that the batter is evenly distributed around the pan. In about 30 seconds it will be cooked. When the edge of the crepe separates from the pan, take a spatula and flip the crepe. Cook on the second side for another 30 seconds. Flip the crepe out of the pan unto a plate. Finish cooking crepes, flipping each onto the platter. It is okay to put them on top of each other so long as you wait a minute or so in between flips.

To serve the blintzes without a filling: Fold each crepe into quarters (folding each one twice, first in half and then in quarters). Arrange the crepes around a serving platter. Add whichever topping or side dishes you wish. Our suggestions include sour cream, Greek yogurt, dates, walnuts or berries.

BLINTZES SERVED WITH CAVIAR

This is a classic holiday dish. After making the blintzes, and placing them on a serving platter, save room in the middle of the platter for a small glass bowl to fill with red caviar or black caviar, or half and half. Circle the outside of the bowl with small cubes of sweet butter. You can serve with a side bowl of sour cream.

BLINTZES WITH MEAT FILLING
(CHICKEN, LAMB, TURKEY OR BEEF)

Ingredients:

About 2 lbs cooked chicken, lamb, beef, or
turkey meat

3 hard-boiled eggs

6 medium onions

1 lb. sliced mushrooms

Salt to taste and black pepper to taste

1 bunch of dill

Directions:

Grind the meat and smash 3 boiled eggs with a fork. Stir-fry 3 medium onions, cubed, until they are wilted. Add in 1/2 lb. sliced mushrooms and continue the stir-fry until the vegetables are crunchy. Mix the meat, eggs, onions and mushrooms together along with 1/2 bunch of chopped dill. (Keep the remaining dill for decorating the serving platter.)

Put a tablespoon of the mix in the center of the blintz. Fold all four sides of the crepe over the mix. Preheat pan with a tablespoon of oil. Place the side with the folds face down into the pan and cook until golden and crunchy (but not burned). Once one side is cooked, turn the blintz over and cook the flat side until golden and crunchy. If you are in a hurry, cook only the folded side.

To garnish:

Slice 1/2 lb. mushrooms into thin slices. Cut 3 onions from top to bottom in half and then cut the halves into thin slices, which will look like half moons. Stir-fry sliced onions until they are wilted. Then add in mushrooms and stir-fry. Use olive oil for the stir-fry as needed. Place the stir-fried mushrooms and onions over the top of each crepe. As an alternative, you can garnish the top of each crepe with a dollop of cranberry sauce.

Blintzes served with squash berry side dish.

BLINTZES WITH BUCKWHEAT AND MUSHROOM FILLING

Ingredients:

1 cup buckwheat	1 lb. mushrooms
2 medium yellow onions	1/4 tsp salt

Directions:

Boil 2 cups of water (you may not use it all). Heat a frying pan on medium flame for 1 minute. Pour dry buckwheat into the dry pan and stir with wooden spoon until the buckwheat is medium brown (about 4-5 minutes). Put the cooked buckwheat into a cooking pot, add 1 cup boiled water, and stir. Place the pot over a medium flame and cook for 15 minutes. Watch the pot and add enough boiling water as needed to keep the buckwheat slightly covered with water. Add in 1/4 tsp salt (do not stir). Keep cooking for five minutes until water is dissolved [cooked through] and the buckwheat is fluffy and dry. Take out of pot and place on a plate so that the buckwheat has a little time to cool down.

While the buckwheat is cooking, prepare the stir-fry. Cut the onions in half top to bottom and then cut thin half moon slices. Slice the mushrooms. Stir-fry onions for about 5 minutes with small amount of olive oil until they are wilted Add in mushrooms and stir-fry together adding olive oil as needed until the vegetables are crunchy. Set aside half of the stir-fry mix for the garnish (see below).

For the blintz filling: Mix half the remaining onions, mushrooms and buckwheat. Salt and pepper to taste. Put a tbsp of the mix in the center of the blintz. Fold all four sides of the crepe over the mix. Preheat pan with a tbsp of oil or butter. Place the side with the folds face down into the pan and cook until golden and crunchy (but not burned). Once one side is cooked, turn the blintz over and cook the flat side until golden and crunchy. If you are in a hurry, you can cook the folded side only.

To garnish: Place the stir-fried mushrooms and onions over the top of each crepe.

NOTE: Blintzes with this filling should be served warm. If you refrigerate, warm before serving.

BLINTZES WITH MUSHROOM FILLING

With this filling, serve the blintz after refrying. Do not refrigerate.

Ingredients:

6 medium onions

1 lb. sliced mushrooms

1 medium cabbage

1 tbsp pine nuts (optional)

2 tbsp olive oil (more, as needed)

Directions:

Cut the onions in half top to bottom and then cut thin half moon slices. Slice the mushrooms. Cut the cabbage in half and finely slice the cabbage. In a deep 10" (or larger) frying pan, stir fry onions. In about 5 minutes add the mushrooms. In another 5 minutes add the cabbage. Mix and stir-fry the vegetables together for about 5 more minutes until the cabbage is wilted. While cooking, add in additional olive oil as needed so that the pan does not burn, but not more than necessary. Salt and pepper as needed. Add in pine nuts and mix.

For the blintz filling: Put a tbsp of the mix in the center of the blintz. Fold all four sides of the crepe over the mix. Preheat pan with a tbsp of oil or butter. Place the side with the folds face down into the pan and cook until golden and crunchy (but not burned). Once one side is cooked, turn the blintz over and cook the flat side until golden and crunchy. If you are in a hurry, cook the folded side only.

To garnish: spoon mushroom/cabbage/onion mix over the top of each blintz. Place a dollop of sour cream with a sprig of dill or parsley on top with a few dried cranberries.

BLINTZES WITH FARMER'S CHEESE FILLING

Ingredients:

1 tablespoon farmer's cheese for each blintz that you plan to serve

1 can of cherry filling or carton of sour
   cream for garnishing the blintzes

Note: These blintzes are served unheated.

Fill each crepe with 1 tbsp of farmer's cheese. Fold each crepe into quarters (folding each one twice, first in half and then in quarters). Place the folded blintzes on a platter. Place a dollop of cherry filling on top of each blintz. An alternative is to place a dollop of sour cream.

BLINTZES WITH SQUASH FILLING

Ingredients:

- 1 cucumber-shaped butter squash, medium or large
- 1 cup dried cranberries
- 1/2 tsp vanilla sugar
- Small carton of sour cream
- Cinnamon

Directions:

Make blintzes as directed above. For the filling, cut cucumber-shaped butter squash into thirds, clean out seeds and set seeds aside for roasting. Remove outside of skins with knife or vegetable peeler. Cut the squash into 1-inch cubes. Bring 1 cup water to a boil in a pot. Put squash cubes into the boiling water and add enough water to cover. After boiling the water, lower the heat to a simmer and cook until it's mashable (about 10 minutes). Remove squash from water. Add 1 cup of dried cranberries and 1/2 teaspoon of vanilla sugar. Set aside the filling until it is warm, not hot. Once the filling is warm, use about 1 tsp to fill each blintz and cook as above.

Garnish each blintz with a dollop of sour cream and a sprinkling of cranberries and cinnamon.

Note: With this filling, serve the blintzes warm or cold.

BLINTZES WITH CRANBERRY FILLING

Ingredients:

- 1 package of fresh cranberries
- 1/4 tsp of vanilla sugar
- Sugar for cooking as recommended on the package of cranberries

Directions:

Cook the cranberries according to package directions, including adding sugar. When berries are cooked, add 1/4 tsp vanilla sugar. Spoon 1 tbsp of cooked cranberries into the middle of a blintz and spread. Roll the blintz closed. No garnish is necessary.

DESSERTS

GREEN APPLE CAKE

Ingredients:

1/4 tsp vanilla sugar

1/2 cup white flour

1/4 tsp baking soda

3 eggs (yolks and whites separated)

a pinch of salt

Graham crackers or ginger snaps, enough to grate and line

1 potato cut in half

3 medium green apples, peeled and cut into 1/2-inch cubes

Directions:

Preheat oven to 375° F. Add a pinch of salt to egg whites. Beat until stiff and you can make peaks. Mix the egg yolks with the sugar. Gently blend the yolk and white mixtures, trying to keep the peaks. Sift flour and baking soda into the mix, add vanilla sugar, and set aside.

Brush a round baking pan with olive oil using 1/2 potato dipped in the oil as a rag. Grate the crackers and sprinkle over bottom and sides of pan so that the bottom surface is well covered.

Place a layer of apple cubes over the bottom of the pan. Without pressing, place the cake mix over the apple layer.

Bake for 45 minutes. If a toothpick comes out clean, it is done.

Serve with whipped cream.

BISCKVIT VANILLA CAKE

Ingredients:

6 eggs

1 cup sugar

1 cup flour

1 tsp vanilla powder

pinch baking soda

Angel food cake mold

Directions:

Preheat oven to 375°F. Separate whites and yolks. Beat egg whites with a pinch of salt until the egg whites are stiff and stand up. Use a large wooden spoon to mix the yolks with the sugar until the sugar is thoroughly dissolved. Carefully fold the egg whites into the yolk mixture. Add the flour and the baking soda and mix well. Add the vanilla powder.

Using a brush or paper towel or half potato, smear the side and bottom of the angel food cake mold with a light covering of olive oil. Pour the mixture into the mold. Bake at 375 for 35 to 45 minutes. The cake will be finished if you insert a toothpick and it comes out clean.

BISCKVIT CHOCOLATE CAKE

Ingredients:

6 eggs

1 cup sugar

1 cup flour

pinch salt

1 tsp vanilla powder

2 tbsp cocoa powder

pinch baking soda

Directions:

Preheat oven to 375°F. Separate whites and yolks. Beat egg whites with a pinch of salt until the egg whites are stiff and stand up. Use a large wooden spoon to mix the yolks with the sugar until the sugar is thoroughly dissolved. Carefully fold the egg whites into the yolk mixture. Add the flour and the baking soda and mix well. Add the vanilla powder and cocoa powder

Using a brush or paper towel or half potato, smear the side and bottom of an angel food cake mold with a light covering of olive oil. Pour the mixture into the mold. Bake at 375°F for 35 to 45 minutes. The cake is finished when you insert a toothpick and it comes out clean.

Bisckvit cake iced and garnished with fruit.

ICING FOR CAKE (CHOCOLATE OR YELLOW CAKE)

Ingredients:

3 egg whites

1 cup sugar

1 baker's chocolate bar (dark, milk or white chocolate)

2 packets (.35 oz. in each packet) of stabilizer for whipping cream

pinch of salt

Lemon, tangerine or mandarin orange

Directions:

Add pinch of salt into egg whites. Beat egg whites until they are extra stiff. Add 2 packets of the stabilizer and mix well into egg whites. Add sugar and mix. Use a knife to spread over the top and side of cake. Shred chocolate and sprinkle lightly over the top of the cake. Shred the yellow skin from the lemon across top of cake being careful to shred only from yellow rind and not deeper.

To decorate top of cake, take 7 segments from a tangerine or mandarin orange. Open each segment in half and arrange the segments evenly over the top of the cake for decoration. In the seam of each segment, put pomegranate seeds or shaved chocolate. To taste, lightly dust the overall top of the cake with cinnamon.

Alternative: just before serving, pour 1/4 cup of orange liqueur or cherry liqueur or fruit juice (pineapple, cranberry or orange) inside the cake hole and let it slosh around the bottom of the cake. It will be absorbed and provide extra flavor. (If you pour the liquid earlier than just before serving, it will make the cake too soggy).

Serves 12

BISCKVIT VANILLA AND CHOCOLATE LAYER CAKE

Ingredients:

6 eggs

1 cup sugar

1 cup flour

1 tsp vanilla powder

pinch baking soda

1 tbsp cocoa powder

Angel food cake mold

Directions:

Preheat oven to 375°F. Separate whites and yolks. Beat egg whites with a pinch of salt until the egg whites are stiff and stand up. Use a large wooden spoon to mix the yolks with the sugar until the sugar is thoroughly dissolved. Carefully fold the egg whites into the yolk mixture. Add the flour, vanilla powder and the baking soda and mix well.

Using a brush or paper towel or half potato, smear the side and bottom of the angel food cake mold with a light covering of olive oil. Take 2/3 of the mix and put into mold, and bake at 375°F for 35 to 45 minutes or until a toothpick comes out clean. Remove cake. This will be used for the vanilla layers.

With the other third of the mix, add the cocoa powder, mix well and put into mold. Bake for about 25 to 35 minutes or until a toothpick comes out clean.

Cut the vanilla cake in half so that there are two layers.

WALNUT CARAMEL FILLING

Ingredients:

3 egg whites

bag of shelled walnuts

pinch of salt

1 lemon

1/2 cup cane sugar

2 cans concentrated milk (14 oz. a can)

2 packets (.35 oz. in each packet) of
stabilizer for whipping cream

Filling for the two bottom layers should be made at least two hours before so that it is not warm when it is spread on the cake.

Directions:

Put cans of the concentrated milk in a pot and fill with enough water so that the can is covered 3/4 high with water. Bring the water to a boil and simmer for 2-1/2 hours. While simmering, add enough water so that the cans are always covered with water. When finished, let the mixture cool and stand until ready to use. The finished mixture will be like caramel.

Cover each layer with caramel (but not the top of the cake). Frost top and sides of cake using frosting on previous page.

To finish the top layer of the cake, use icing below.

SOUR CREAM ICING FOR
CHOCOLATE OR YELLOW CAKE

Ingredients:

1 cup sour cream (or light sour cream)

1 tbsp cane sugar

1 cup nuts (pistachio, walnuts. pine nuts or
cashews)

2 cups fresh berries (raspberries,
blueberries, blackberries or any
combination)

1 tsp vanilla powder

Directions:

Place the layer on top of the cake. If cut, put cut side up. Mix sour cream with sugar and vanilla powder. Cover top of cake with sour cream mix. Over the sour cream layer, decorate with a layer of the berries. Sprinkle nuts on top of the fruit.

Note: this topping is best used to finish off a cut cake, like this half chocolate cake, rather than an uncut top.

Serves 6-8

Yellow and chocolate Bisckvit layer cake.

HONEY CAKE

What Rosh Hashanah meal would be complete without a honey cake for a sweet new year! Here is a traditional favorite.

Ingredients:

1 tbsp olive oil	vanilla sugar (to sprinkle with)
1/2 lb. walnuts, cracked	1 lemon (skin washed and dried)
1 cup honey	1 potato
4 tbsp butter (room temperature)	pinch of salt
1 cup sifted flour	3 eggs (separate whites and yolks)

Optional: 1/2 lb. raisins, or dried or fresh cooked cranberries

Directions:

Preheat oven to 375°F. Put honey in a large mixing bowl. Add the eggs, a pinch of salt, walnuts, fruit, sugar and mix. Fold in butter and olive oil. Put sifted flour in and mix well.

Bake in an angel food cake or Bundt pan. To prepare pan, cut the potato in half. Put olive oil in pan by dipping the potato in the olive oil and using it as a rag to lightly coat the bottom and sides of the pan. You may coat the pan with butter but the cake turns darker with it. Pour or scoop the mixture into the pan. It will smooth around by itself. Grate the skin of the lemon over the top of the mix.

Bake for 45 minutes. If a toothpick comes out clean, it is done.

Honey cake decorated with orange slices and powdered sugar.

CHOCOLATE CHIP AND WALNUT COOKIES

Ingredients:

1 stick unsalted butter (leave out for an hour to soften)

3 tbls sour cream

3 tbls sugar

1/4 cup dark chocolate chips

1/4 cup white chocolate chips

1 cup chopped walnuts

1/2 pack of vanilla sugar

1/2 cup uncooked cooking oats (not steel cut)

1/2 cup flour

1/8 tsp cinnamon

Directions:

Preheat oven to 375°F. Put butter, sugar and sour cream in large mixing bowl and mix together. Add remaining ingredients and mix until smooth.

Take a soupspoon-sized lump of dough and roll into a ball about an inch in diameter. Make sure that the mix easily separates from your hand; if it does not, add enough flour to the mix so that the ball does not stick to your hand. Place balls on greased baking sheet. Leave about 2 inches space between balls.

Bake in oven for 20 minutes. Check to see if toothpick comes clean when inserted into ball. Finished cookies should be golden brown.

Chocolate chip walnut oatmeal cookies

CHOCOLATE COVERED ORANGES/FRUITS

Ingredients:

Tangerine segments, strawberries, banana slices, large blueberries, or apple slices

Flat bar of baker's dark, milk or white chocolate.

Directions:

Melt the chocolate slowly in small pot over very, very low heat and stir while melting.

Rinse the fruit and dry thoroughly. Put on pieces of paper towel and let sit to make sure outside of fruit is thoroughly dry.

For chocolate dip: Place a toothpick (or two) in the fruit. Angle the chocolate inside the pot with one hand, with the other hand dip the fruit into the chocolate. Hold dipped fruit over the melted chocolate so that it drips the excess. Place dipped fruit on tin foil placed on a cookie sheet. Do this for all pieces.

Place chocolate fruit in the refrigerator until it is chilled (about 30 minutes).

You can dip any of these fruits in any color chocolate. For the larger pieces, you can dip twice for different colors, for example, dip a strawberry in chocolate, chill and then dip part of it in white chocolate.

Chocolate covered oranges.

YOM KIPPUR

Smoked salmon rolls.

STARTERS

SMOKED SALMON ROLLS WITH CUCUMBER

Ingredients:

½ lb sliced smoked salmon (ask for long slices)

2 cucumbers about 6" long

8 small cherry tomatoes

8 springs of parsley

Directions:

Wash and skin the cucumbers. Slice the cucumber lengthwise into 4 quarters.

Wrap a long piece of smoked salmon around the cucumber quarter by rolling it around the slice. If you think the slice is too long, cut it in half.

Place the rolls on a serving plate in a circle around it. Spread sprig of parsley on top of the roll, place a cherry tomato on top of the parsley so that the parsley sprig shows under the tomato. With a toothpick, pin the cherry tomato to the roll.

Serves 8

BEET AND CARROT SLAW

This colorful and crunchy salad is a perfect complement to a fish course.

Ingredients:

1 apple, peeled and shredded in large hole of shredder

1/2 cabbage, sliced thin

2 beets, shredded in large hole of shredder

3 carrots, shredded in large hole of shredder

1 whole lemon, cut in half

1 cup walnuts (optional)

1 cup dried cranberries (optional)

Directions:

Mix all ingredients thoroughly together. May be refrigerated for several days.

Before serving, mix in a smattering of olive oil and then serve.

Serves 4-6

Fish in tomato sauce.

MAIN COURSES

FISH IN TOMATO SAUCE

Ingredients:

2 lbs filleted fish (whitefish or mahi-mahi) cut into four pieces

1 large carrot, shredded

1 large white onion, chopped

salt, pepper

1 small can tomato paste

olive oil

6 bay leaves

Directions:

Preheat oven to 350°F. Heat frying pan and cover inside of pan with thin coating of olive oil. Add chopped onion and stir. When onion turns golden, add shredded carrot. Stir and fry together for 1 minute. Sprinkle salt and pepper on vegetables and add the bay leaves and tomato paste and stir. Now add 1 and 1/2 cups water and mix.

Place the fish in a glass baking dish. Spoon vegetable mix over and around the fish. Cover the dish with tin foil. Bake for 1 hour.

To serve: can be served hot or cold but we think it tastes better when chilled. To serve cold, chill fish in refrigerator for several hours. Serve garnished with sliced lemon, parsley, shredded carrots or horseradish.

Serves 4

Stuffed peppers.

STUFFED PEPPERS

Ingredients:

1 and 1/2 pounds of ground beef, turkey, lamb or chicken

3 medium sized yellow onions

3 medium sized carrots

A few stalks of parsley

1/4 cup brown rice

8 medium sized peppers (green and/or red and/or yellow)

1 small can tomato paste

A few bay leaves

Salt and pepper

Directions:

Preheat oven to 375°F. The peppers will be baked in a pot or pan at least 4 or 5 inches deep.

Preheat large frying pan by putting in enough oil to cover the surface of the pan and heat over low flame. Chop the onion into small pieces. Put chopped onion into frying pan , mix in with the oil, and let cook over medium heat. In the meantime, shred three carrots (use large holed shredder). When onion becomes golden, add carrots. Continue cooking together for 2 minutes. Rinse and chop parsley finely. Add 1/2 the chopped parsley to the cooking pan, sprinkle salt and pepper, stir to mix all together, then turn off flame.

Rinse fresh peppers. Cut a "lid" around the top of the pepper (approximately two inches in diameter) and remove lid. To make the meat mix for stuffing, first place the chopped meat in a large mixing bowl. Chop the lid portion of the pepper (but not the stem) and add to the ground meat. Mix in half of the cooked onion/parsley/carrot mix, and also add the uncooked brown rice. Sprinkle salt and ground pepper and mix all together well. Using a spoon, stuff each pepper with the meat mix, being careful not to break the pepper. Place stuffed peppers tightly together in a baking pan.

Warm the remaining onion/parsley/carrot mix in the pan over medium flame. After the mix is heated and while flame is on, add the tomato paste, the remaining chopped parsley, the bay leaves, 2 cups water and mix together. Once mixed, turn off flame. Spoon the mix over the stuffed peppers and around the peppers. Make sure that the peppers have at least one inch of covering over the top. Cover the entire pot with aluminum foil and bake for about 1 1/2 hours.

Serves 8

Baked whitefish garnished with lemon and orange slices.

BAKED WHITEFISH

Ingredients:

4 lbs. whole whitefish (or salmon/northern pike)

1/2 cup mayonnaise

1 large yellow onion

1 lemon

Black pepper

1 bunch of scallions, diced thin

4 large cloves of garlic (optional)

Fresh dill, enough for about two cups of diced dill

Directions:

Preheat oven to 400°F. Rinse fish. Slice fish lengthwise down the belly side from below the head to top of the tail. When the slice is made, spread open the fish and you will see the backbone. Make a crosswise cut on the backbone below the head so that there is enough space to slide a few fingers under the top of the backbone. Using your fingers, remove the backbone by pulling it away from the flesh of the fish all the way from the neck to the tailfin. With the backbone pulled out, the head of the fish and a small piece of tail will still be intact.

At this point the fish will lie flat against the counter, skin the side on the counter. Pull away any other bones that were left on the fish. Run your fingers down the inside of the fish. You should not feel any bones in the flesh. Rinse the inside and outside of the fish with cold water. Then, squeeze the excess water from the fish. Place opened fish backside down into a baking pan brushed with oil and that is long enough to hold the entire fish.

Chop the dill. Peel skin from the onion. Cut onion in half and then cut thin slices (they will be in a half moon shape). Cut lemon in half. Squeeze juice from one half the lemon over the entire fish being careful not to squeeze seeds on the fish. Use a teaspoon to dig out the pulp from the lemon and place it over the fish. Sprinkle black pepper on the fish.

Place onion slices over one side for the entire length of the fish flesh. Place scallions on top of the onions. Fold fish closed; make sure that the closure is a neat as possible with the onions inside the fish. Squeeze juice from the other half lemon over the top of the fish.

Crush the garlic cloves over the diced dill and mix together so the garlic is evenly distributed within the dill. Pile the dill/garlic mixture evenly over the top of the fish, except for the head and the fins of the tail. Spoon mayonnaise over the top, smushing the mayonnaise into the dill mix.

Place a piece of tin foil over the fish and wrap it to the edge of the pan. The tin foil should not be touching the fish, just the edges of the pan. Bake at 400°F for about 30 minutes and then take away the tin foil. Cook for another 30 minutes. Remove from oven and set aside to cool for an hour.

To serve: place fish on serving plate being careful to keep the fish intact. Decorate the edges of the plate with sliced citrus fruits (lemons, oranges or limes or any combination).

Serves 6-8

In preparation: one rolled out dough ball about 12 inches in diameter with cherries placed around part of the rim.

DESSERTS

CHERRY PYRAMID CAKE

Note: This cake must be made a day in advance of serving.

Ingredients for dough:

- Measure 3 and 2/3 cups of flour
- 4 cans of cherry pie filling
- 1 cup of sour cream (in measuring cup for liquids)
- 2 8-ounce sticks of margarine
- Up to 1 tablespoon white distilled vinegar
- 1/2 teaspoon baking soda
- Pinch of vanilla powder

Ingredients for icing:

- 4 cups of sour cream (2% or whole milk)
- 1-1/2 cups of cane sugar (in measure cup for liquids)
- Sprinkle of vanilla powder
- 2 cups walnut, broken into small pieces
- Up to 4 packs of whipping cream stabilizer (at .35 oz. a pack).

Directions:

Place flour on a flat rolling board or kitchen counter. Put margarine from refrigerator in the middle of the flour and dice margarine into small pieces. Add one cup of sour cream in the middle of the flour and diced margarine. Place the baking soda in the tablespoon measure and fill to the top of the tablespoon with the vinegar. Put the vinegar and baking soda into the sour cream. Knead together the flour, margarine, sour cream, vinegar and baking soda. (This is messy work but your kids will love it!) The mixture is ready when the ingredients are thoroughly mixed and the dough is dry enough to leave your hands without sticking.

Cut the dough into 10 parts and shape each part into a ball. Each ball will be rolled to become a cherry roll.

Chill the dough for two hours. In the meantime, preheat oven at 375°F. When the dough is chilled, take out and prepare to make rolls by first sprinkling a baking board (or counter top) with flour. Place each ball on a rolling board and roll it into a circle with a 12-inch diameter.

Recipe continues on page 60

In preparation: starting to roll up the dough.

Place the cherries around the edge for half of one dough circle (see picture above). Roll up the dough from the cherry side first, pinching the end of the roll as needed to make sure the cherries stay inside. Roll the dough in as tight a roll as possible.

In preparation: rolling and pinching the dough closed as it turns over.

In preparation: completing the roll up of the dough.

After making five rolls, bake them at 375°F until the rolls are light gold. While the first group is baking, roll the other five rolls and then bake. Cool the rolls for a few hours. You can bake the rolls a day or so in advance (but do not refrigerate, or they get gritty).

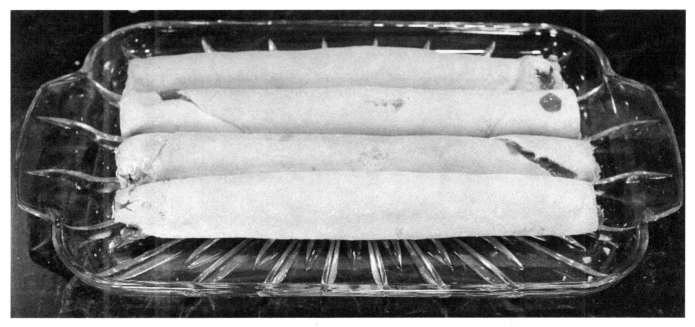

Picture shows four parallel rolls of equal length. Note that longer rolls are snipped at the end to make all four rolls of equal length.

Preparation of the frosting and finishing the cake:

Place four cups of sour cream in a bowl, add a sprinkling of vanilla sugar, add the whipping cream stabilizer and mix with spoon. Start with 2 packs of stabilizer and add enough as needed so that the cream forms stiff peaks. Mix for about 3 minutes or until the cream has the consistency of cake frosting. Put in freezer for 10 to 20 minutes (but do not freeze).

Place 4 of the baked cherry rolls on a serving dish, placing them in parallel position right next to each other. The rolls should be the same length. If a roll is longer than the others, cut the end to match the length of the others. *(See picture.)*

Take chilled cream out of the freezer and immediately start to frost the cake. With a frosting spatula (or flat knife) apply about a 1/4 of the frosting to the top of the first layer of cherry rolls, just enough to cover the top of the rolls with a layer of frosting, but not more. Sprinkle a layer of walnuts on top of the first layer of frosting. Place 3 cherry rolls on top of the first frosted layer. Position the three rolls lengthwise so that they are centered over the first layer of four rolls. Frost the second layer and sprinkle that layer with walnuts.

Center two cherry rolls on top of the second layer, frost and again sprinkle with walnuts. Finish by centering and placing the 10th roll on top of the cake. Frost the 10th roll first and then all sides of the cake. After frosting, decorate the side of the cake with either nuts, small berries, lemon wedges, shredded chocolate, small candies or lemon zest in any pattern or amount that you wish. (See picture for an example but you can use your imagination for any style decoration you like. Sometimes we make a Jewish star with berries). This is a fun job that children may enjoy.

Chill the decorated cake in the refrigerator for at least a day before serving. The cake may be chilled in the refrigerator up to three days in advance of serving.

In preparation: layers of the rolls first frosted
then sprinkled with walnuts.

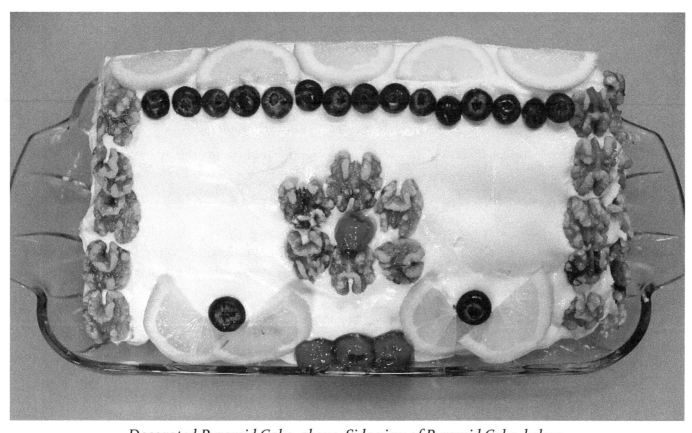

Decorated Pyramid Cake, above. Side view of Pyramid Cake, below.

BAKED SQUASH APPLES

This healthy dish works as either a sweet side dish at dinner or dessert.

Ingredients:

1 butternut squash

Six medium-sized apples

1 cup shelled walnuts

1/2 tsp of honey per apple

Directions:

Preheat oven to 350°F.

Cut a butter squash crosswise into six one-inch slices. Place slices in boiling water and turn heat down so that the slices simmer for 5 minutes until soft. Turn off heat. Check to see that squash is soft and then dispose of squash water

Core through half the center of each apple. Put walnuts inside the center and drizzle honey over the walnuts. Bake the apples at 350°F until apple flesh softens (about 15 minutes).

Place each squash slice on the service platter. Gently scoop out about 1/4-inch round "bed" from the center of the slice on which to place the apple. Place an apple on the squash bed.

To serve: You may serve this dish hot or cold. If served hot, garnish with berries or drizzled chocolate. If served cold, you may choose to serve with whipped cream, ice cream or frozen yoghurt.

Serves 6

Baked apple on squash.

SUCCOT

SOUPS

BORSCHT WITH CHICKEN OR BEEF

Ingredients:

If chicken: 1 whole chicken, cut into 8 pieces. (You can remove the skin)

If beef: 2 lbs short ribs

1 large (or two medium) potatoes

1 green cabbage

1 large carrot (or 2 medium carrots)

2 medium or one large beet

1 pinch of parsley or dill

3-5 cloves of garlic (to taste)

1 large onion, peeled

1 small can of tomato paste

1 green pepper

Directions:

Place the meat into a pot and cover with water. Bring water to a boil. Once the water has boiled, empty the pot and rinse the meat with cold water.

Fill a large soup pot halfway with water and bring to a boil. Once the water has boiled, add the rinsed meat into the pot. Add the onion, then lower the heat so the water stays simmering and cook for 40 minutes slightly uncovered.

While cooking, slice the vegetables. Chop the parsley into fine pieces. On top of the parsley, mince the garlic cloves. Peel the beets (you can use a knife or a vegetable peeler). Shred the beets and the carrots using the large hole side of the shredder. Quarter the green pepper, clean out the seed, and then slice the quarter into very thin slices. Cut the cabbage into quarters and slice into very thin slices. Peel and slice the potato and cut into 1/2-inch cubes.

Remove the cooked onion from the pot (after 20 minutes and while the meat is still cooking). After 40 minutes, add the beets into the pot and cook for five minutes. Then, add the carrots, green pepper, potatoes, cabbage, and tomato paste and cook another 15 minutes. Add salt and pepper to taste. Turn off flame and add the garlic and parsley. Cover the pot, let sit for 30 minutes and then serve.

Optional Garnish: you can put a dollop of sour cream or Greek yoghurt on top of each serving.

Serves 6-8

PUMPKIN SOUP

Ingredients:

1 large fresh pumpkin with a stem, nicely rounded

3 large onions

Nutmeg, ginger, salt and pepper to taste

Directions:

Cut a circle around the top of the pumpkin and its stem so you can lift a round lid from it and wide enough to use the lid like a pot cover. Scrape the seeds from the top and set aside. Using a large metal soupspoon, scrape the seeds from inside the pumpkin. Once the pumpkin is free of seed, use the spoon to scrape long pieces of pumpkin flesh from the inside. Scrape enough to fill a 5 qt. pot.

Cut the onions in half and then make thin slices. In a frying pan, use olive oil to cook the onions for about 10 minutes. Fill a large soup pot halfway with water and bring to a boil. Add 1/4 tsp of salt. Place the onions and pumpkin flesh into the pot, bring to a boil and then lower heat to a simmer. Cook until the pumpkin is soft and can be pureed.

Remove the vegetables from the pot. They will be hot, so let them cool down for a few minutes. Puree vegetables.

Optional: Add up to a can of unsweetened condensed milk for a creamy consistency. Add salt, pepper, nutmeg and cinnamon to taste. Soup can be made in advance and heated before serving.

To serve: Place the hot soup back into the pumpkin and cover with the pumpkin top. Bring the pumpkin to the center of the table. This can be done in advance of your guests being seated so that the pumpkin looks like a centerpiece. When ready to serve, lift the lid and spoon soup into a bowl. Garnish with a dollop of sour cream, Greek yoghurt, shredded ginger or nuts (walnuts or pecans).

Serves 8

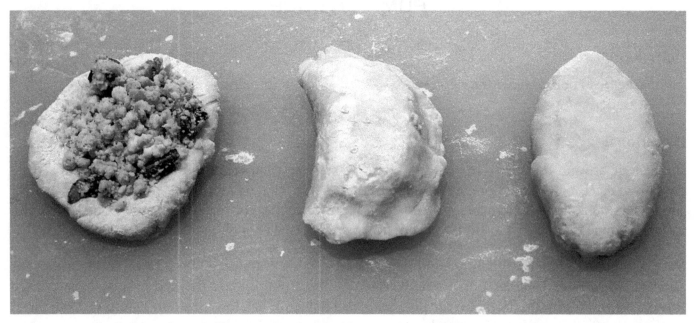

A rolled knish with filling, a pinched half-moon knish, and a knish ready to cook.

A plate of knishes or zrahzees ready to serve.

MAIN DISHES OR SIDE DISHES

KNISH OR ZRAHZEE
(POTATO STUFFED WITH CHICKEN OR MEAT)

Ingredients:

About 2 cups of cooked meat (chicken, turkey, beef or lamb)

3 hard-boiled eggs

3 raw eggs

2 medium onions (or one large)

Salt to taste

1 tbsp chopped dill or parsley

Up to 3 cups flour

5 large or 10 medium potatoes

Pinch of baking soda

Up to 5 tbsp olive oil

1/2 lb. sliced, diced mushrooms

Directions:

Peel potatoes, cut in half and boil with 1/4 tsp salt until soft (~ 10 minutes). Empty pot and rinse potatoes in a colander. Mash the potatoes. Set aside.

Grind the meat and hard-boiled eggs and place in a mixing bowl. Dice the onion into small pieces and sauté in 3 tablespoons of olive oil. After five minutes, add in sliced mushroom and sauté for another five minutes. Add additional oil as needed. Remove sautéed vegetables and add to meat and egg mix.

Make the mashed potato dough by first adding three raw eggs to the mashed potato mix. Add 1 cup of flour and mix into potatoes. Mix in second cup of flour. Knead mix together to make a ball of dough. The dough is ready when it is dry enough so that it does not stick to your hand. Add more flour as needed to obtain the right degree of dryness.

Take about 1/4 of the dough and roll it out into a long cucumber shape about 2-inches wide. Slice the dough into 1/2-inch slices. Flatten each piece into a round shape about 3 inches in diameter and about 1/4-inch thick. In the middle of each dough disk, place a tablespoon of the meat filling. Fold the dough over into a half moon shape and pinch the sides shut. Then, fold over the pinched side and knead the zrahzee so that it is a rounded flat oval shape. (See picture for sequence of forming the zrahzee.) Place the zrahzees on a plate so that the pinched side of each is on the bottom.

Heat frying pan and put in enough olive oil to generously cover the bottom of the pan. Seam side down, fry the zrahzee until the underside is golden. Flip over the zrahzee and fry the second side until it is also golden. Take zrahzees out of pan and drain on a paper towel.

To serve: place zrahzees on a serving plate. Garnish with fresh vegetables or apple sauce or serve plain.

This recipe yields about 28 pieces. 1-2 pieces are enough for a lunch or dinner main course.

BUTTERNUT SQUASH KASHA

Ingredients:

1 cucumber-shaped butter squash

1 can of sweetened concentrated milk

1/4 tsp of vanilla sugar

1/2 cup of rice (white or brown)

1/2 cup of raisins or dried cranberries

Directions:

Cut the squash into thirds; clean out seeds (you can also set the seeds aside for roasting). Remove the squash skin with knife or vegetable peeler. Cut the squash into 1-inch cubes.

Cook rice as directed on package until firm. Add 1 can of milk and the squash cubes to the rice and continue cooking for about 10 minutes or until rice is fluffy. You may add water to cover the mix. When cooked, add the dried fruit and mix. Serve cold or warm. Sprinkle the top with nuts (walnuts, pecans, almonds or pistachios).

BAKED BUTTERNUT SQUASH OR PUMPKIN WITH APPLES

Ingredients:

6 small butternut squashes or pumpkin

6 small green apples

6 tbls roasted walnuts

6 tsp honey

Directions:

Cut a circle around the top of the squash (wide enough to spoon in food). Remove and discard the lid. Take out the seeds using a large soupspoon to scrape them free. Core the apples. Place the cored apples inside the squash or pumpkin. Place some nuts inside the core of the apple. Then dribble about a teaspoon of honey over the nuts. Bake at 350°F until squash is soft. Remove from oven. Sprinkle small amount of brown sugar and cinnamon over the top.

Serves 6

EGGPLANT STUFFED WITH CHICKEN

Ingredients:

2 eggplants about 8 inches long

2 cups ground cooked chicken (can use baked chicken leftovers).

1/2 onion diced

Salt and pepper to taste

1/4 cup of chopped dill

1 large Portobello mushroom, diced into cubes

To prepare the stuffing:

Heat the olive oil in a frying pan for about 1 minute over medium heat. Stir the chicken, mushrooms and onions in the heated olive oil, sprinkle in black pepper and salt. Stir the stuffing mix in the pan for about five minutes until onions are golden. Stir in the chopped dill.

To prepare the eggplant:

Preheat oven to 350°F.

Cut off the ends of each eggplant (about a 1/2-inch slice off each end). Cut each eggplant crosswise into four equal slices, each slice about 2 inches thick. Place each slice on an oiled or buttered baking pan.

Scoop out eggplant pulp inside from each slice so that you can fill each slice with the stuffing. Be careful not to scoop through the bottom of the slice. Bake eggplant slices until pulp pierces easily with a fork for about 10 minutes.

Remove from oven and let stand for about 10 minutes until the slices are cool enough to work with. Place stuffing in each eggplant cup, enough of the stuffing in each one so that it is topped off with a small mound of stuffing. Place a heaping teaspoon of mayonnaise on the top of each stuffing mound. Put stuffed slices back in oven for five minutes or until the mayonnaise is melted but not brown. Serve hot.

Serves 8

RUSSIAN FRIED CHICKEN

Ingredients:

One 4-5 lb. whole Cornish hen (can substitute one 4-5 pound whole chicken cut in half) Salt and pepper

Enough dill to make 3/4 cup diced dill

2 garlic cloves

1/3 cup olive oil

Directions:

Cut chicken in half and place in a thin plastic bag. Use a mallet or rolling pin to pound each half flat. Rub a couple of shakes of salt on both sides of the chicken; sprinkle pepper on the skin. Set aside for thirty minutes to let seasoning seep in.

Preheat large frying pan for a couple of minutes on medium heat. Pour 1/3 cup olive oil in heated pan. Place 2 half chickens skin side down in pan. Place a large pot filled with water over the top of the chickens so that they are pressed down. Fry for about 15 minutes and then turn over and fry for another 10 to 15 minutes until chicken is browned.

While the chickens are frying, dice the dill. Squeeze the garlic over the dill. Sprinkle dill over the chicken and serve.

Serves 4-6

Russian fried chicken with tomato and starfruit decoration.

Squash berry dessert.

DESSERTS

SQUASH BERRY DESSERT

Ingredients:

1 cucumber-shaped butter squash, about 6-8 inches

1 package blueberries

1 package raspberries

brown sugar and cinnamon to sprinkle

1 lemon (shred the skin)

1 large package of Greek yoghurt or sour cream

1/2 cup walnuts

Directions:

Preheat oven to 375°F. Wash and cut the squash into rounds that are about 1 inch thick. Remove seeds taking care not to break the rounds. There will be a hole in the middle after the seeds are removed.

Cover a cookie sheet with aluminum foil. Preheat the covered sheet. Place rounds of squash on the cookie sheet and bake for 10 minutes until soft but not browned. Remove sheet from oven and set aside. At this point, you can continue to prepare the dessert to serve it warm or you can refrigerate the squash and serve cold at a later time.

Rinse berries and pat dry. For each serving dish, place a squash round on a dessert plate. Drop dollops of Greek yoghurt or sour cream in the middle hole of the squash slice. Place walnuts around edge of yoghurt or sour cream. Decorate top of squash slice and edge of plate with blueberries and raspberries. Wash and dry the lemon, grate a little skin over the dollops of cream. Sprinkle with brown sugar and/ or cinnamon.

Serves 6-8

APPLE KUGEL

This versatile dish can be served warm or cold, for breakfast, as a light lunch, or for dessert.

Ingredients:

1 lb. sweet farmer's cheese (can use reduced-fat cheese)

1 cup raisins

3 medium apples, peeled and cut into 1 inch pieces

1/4 tsp vanilla sugar

3 large eggs

13-15 large pieces of walnuts

2 tbls sugar

1 cup flour

1 cup of berries (raspberries, blueberries or blackberries or any combination to make 1 cup)

Directions:

Preheat oven to 350°F.

Mix cheese, eggs, apples, raisins, sugar and vanilla sugar into a large mixing bowl. Then mix in flour. Spread the mixture evenly into a pie pan that has been greased with olive oil. Place the walnuts in a circle around the top of the mix. Bake in oven for about 1 hour.

Start checking for completeness after about 45 minutes. The kugel is done when it is golden brown and a toothpick comes out clean after it is inserted into the cake.

To serve: Serve warm, or chill and serve cold. You may decorate with berries, nuts, lemon zest or sliced lemons.

Serves 8-10

Apple kugel.

CHANUKAH

Chanukah occurs in the winter when most of Russia's vegetation is in colorless hibernation. To add to the holiday cheer, many people used fruits and vegetables that were available. In the Russian tradition, garlic is an important winter ingredient to protect against influenza.

The most well-known Chanukah recipe is for latkes. This is a Russian Chanukah classic possibly because potatoes were one of the few vegetables available in winter. In Russian, latkes were called either drahnikee (potato latke) or oladee (fruit latke). The following favorite latke recipes may be served either for breakfast, lunch or dinner.

Potato latkes served with sliced apples and sour cream.

LATKES

POTATO LATKES

Utensils:

- 2 frying pans, 1 at least 10-inch, both skillets or non-stick pans
- 1 4-sided grater

- 2 glass or stainless steel mixing bowls
- 1 wooden spoon

Ingredients:

- 4 large potatoes
- 3 large yellow onion
- 2 large Portobello mushrooms (one for cooking, the other for decoration)
- salt and pepper

- 1 cup of olive oil
- 1 tsp fresh dill cut in tiny pieces
- 3 tbsp flour
- 2 eggs

To make latkes:

Preheat a 10-inch skillet using just enough olive oil to cover the bottom of the pan. Peel the potatoes. Shred them by hand using the shredder's largest opening (to keep them crunchy.) Peel and hand shred one onion, again using the largest opening. Try to shred potatoes and onion very quickly so that the potatoes don't change color and the onions retain their juice. Peel one mushroom by taking off the top layer of skin, shred and mix together with onion and potatoes.

Put shredded potatoes, mushroom and onions into one of the mixing bowls, add salt and pepper to taste and the cut dill. With a wooden spoon, mix in 1 tbsp of flour and 2 eggs. Then add 1 or 2 tbsp flour or more while constantly mixing. There should be enough flour added so that it holds together in a ball but is not too hard. *Do not add too much flour.*

To make vegetable mix:

Peel and slice the second onion in half. Then slice each half in thin slices. Slice one Portobello mushroom in thin slices also. Place the onion and Portobello slices in a frying pan.

Note: You will be cooking the latke and vegetable mixes in separate pans at the same time.

To cook the latke mix:

Preheat pan on medium flame for 2 minutes. Add a dollop of olive oil to second pan and place on medium to high flame. Take a tbsp of the mix, place it into the second pan and flatten it. You can put more than one latke in the pan if they are not touching. After the latke(s) is browned on one side (2-3 mins.), flip it over and cook it for another 2 mins. Cooking time depends on amounts and texture of the ingredients so you may want to take a small bite of one to see if it's done. Each time you cook another round of latkes, add in another dollop of olive oil as needed to keep the pan properly greased. After cooking, place each latke on a paper towel for a few seconds to drain the oil, then flip and drain the other side (it is juicier without draining but many people don't want to eat that much oil).

To cook the vegetables:

Heat the vegetable pan and gently cook the vegetables, stirring from time to time. They will be done when they turn gold. Place on paper towels to pat and drain.

To serve: place the latkes on a plate (preferably a glass one so that you can see how colorful they are). Add a tbsp of the onion/mushroom mix on top of each latke.

To add more color or variety: Put a dollop of sour cream on top of each latke. You may want to add a tsp of black caviar or red caviar on top of the sour cream. You may prefer to put a tbsp of applesauce on top of the latkes. Another alternative is a tbsp of cranberry sauce.

Serves 10-12

FRESH APPLE SAUCE

Ingredients:

- 4 apples
- 1/4 tsp vanilla
- 1/4 tsp cinnamon

Directions:

Peel the apples, cut in quarters and place in a food processor. Add the cinnamon and vanilla.

To serve: put a tbsp of the mix on top of each latke.

FRESH CRANBERRY SAUCE

Ingredients:

1 package of fresh cranberries

1 cup sugar

1 fresh orange

Directions:

Grate orange rind and set aside. Wash cranberries well. Place them in a food processor with the sugar and 1/4 of the orange. Mix until it is ground but not reduced to juice. It should be firm. Add in more sugar a bit at a time if the sauce is not sweet enough. Sprinkle the freshly grated rind on top and serve.

APPLE LATKES

Ingredients:

1 green apple

1 egg

1 plum

3 tbls flour or 1-1/2 tbsp flour and 1-1/2 tbsp oatmeal

1 tsp sugar

1/4 tsp vanilla sugar

pinch of baking soda

1 tbsp sour cream or any yoghurt

dab of butter

several tbls of olive oil

Directions:

Do not peel the apple. Shred the apple using the large shredder holes. Cut the plum into thin strips. Mix together. Add the sugar and egg. Add the sour cream or yoghurt. Add the flour (or flour/oatmeal combination), vanilla sugar and baking soda. Mix together.

Put in as much olive oil as needed to cover the bottom of the pan and preheat pan until just bubbling. Add a dab of butter for taste. Wet the tip of a knife and put a drop of water from the knife on the side of the pan. If the water sizzles, the pan is ready. Use a soupspoon and take a clump of mix, place in pan and use a spatula to flatten. Fry on one side until light brown (about 2 minutes).

Use a spatula to flip the latke and fry the other side. Take the latke out of the pan and place on paper towel to drain oil. Then flip and drain the other side. Serve with cinnamon, sliced orange or berries can be put on top with ice cream, whipped cream and or shredded chocolate or lemon skin.

Serves 4

CABBAGE LATKES

Ingredients:

1-1/2 cups shredded green cabbage

1/4 cup shredded onions

1 egg

1/2 cup shredded Portobello mushroom

2 tbsp flour (or 1 tbsp oatmeal/1 tbsp flour combined)

Directions:

Shred the vegetables using the large shredder holes, and mix. Add egg. Add the flour or flour/oatmeal combination. Salt and pepper to taste. Mix well. Heat pan over medium heat and when hot, add tbsp of olive oil. Put in as much oil as needed to cover the bottom of the pan. Heat until just bubbling and add a dab of butter (for taste).

To determine when the pan is hot enough, wet the tip of a knife and put a drop of water from the knife on the side of the pan; if the water sizzles, the pan is ready. Use a soupspoon and take a clump of mix, place in pan and use a spatula to flatten. Fry on one side until light brown (about 2 minutes). Use a spatula to flip the latke and fry the other side until light brown. Take the latke out of the pan and place on paper towel to drain oil. Then flip to drain the other side.

To serve: put a dollop of sour cream on top, or a leaf of parsley or dill.

Serves 4

CARROT AND ZUCCHINI LATKES

Ingredients:

1 carrot

1 zucchini

1 small yellow onion

1 egg

1 tbsp sour cream or any yoghurt

dab of butter

3 tbsp flour (or 1/2 tbsp flour and 1-1/2 tbsp oatmeal combined)

olive oil as needed

pinch of baking soda

Directions:

Peel carrots and peel zucchini. Shred the vegetables using the large shredder holes. Mix together. Add 1 tbsp of shredded onion. Add egg. Add the flour or flour/oatmeal combination. Salt and pepper to taste.

Add a pinch of baking soda. Mix together. Heat pan over medium flame; when hot, add 1 tbsp of olive oil. Put in as much oil as needed to cover the bottom of the pan. Heat until just bubbling and add a dab of butter (for taste). Wet the tip of a knife and put a drop of water from the knife on the side of the pan. If the water sizzles, the pan is ready.

Use a soupspoon and take a clump of mix, place in pan and use a spatula to flatten. Fry on one side until light gold (~ 2 minutes). Use a spatula to flip the latke and fry the other side. Take latke out of pan and place on paper towel to drain oil. Then flip to drain on other side.

Serves 6

Tongue and potato platter.

MAIN COURSES AND SIDE DISHES

TONGUE AND POTATO PLATTER

Ingredients:

1 regular tongue or two baby tongues

6 long potatoes, washed

2 large onions

1 tbls of chopped dill

1/2 tsp of olive oil

6 bay leaves

1 tsp of whole peppercorns

1/2 tsp salt

2 large cloves of garlic, peeled

bunch of parsley

Directions:

Preheat oven to 375°F. Rinse the meat. Place the meat into a large soup pot and fill the pot until it the water is about 2 inches from the top. Peel and place the onions in the pot. Put the bay leaves, peppercorns, salt, garlic gloves and parsley into the pot. Bring water to a boil, lower the flame, cover the pot and let water simmer.

In about two hours, check to see if the tongue is cooked by either following the directions that came with the tongue or check by tasting a tiny piece from the end. If ready, the skin should easily peel off. When cooked, remove the tongue from the liquid. Set aside for 10 minutes until it is cool enough to handle. Peel the skin and then slice the tongue crosswise into thin slices. Cover the slices with tin foil to keep warm while the potatoes are cooking.

Slice the potatoes lengthwise into four long quarters. Rub the face of each slice with a little salt. Mix together the chopped dill, crushed garlic and olive oil. Spread the mix across the face of each potato slice. Place potatoes face up on a baking sheet covered with foil. Bake the potatoes until soft (about 20 minutes).

To serve: Place the tongue and potato slices on a platter. One way is to alternate circles of potato slices and tongue slices. Garnish with dollops of horseradish in the middle of the platter or on slices of tongue. If you serve with green vegetables in the middle of the platter such as broccoli bunches, this dish is a complete meal.

Serves 6

CHICKEN SALAD OLIVIER

Ingredients:

1 lb. chicken breasts

1 large green apple

1/2 lb. frozen snap green beans

2 large kosher pickles

3 medium-sized boiled potatoes

5 hard boiled eggs

1 large cucumber (skinned or unskinned)

1/2 cup sour cream (or light sour cream)

1/2 cup mayonnaise (or light mayonnaise)

1 tsp fresh dill, sliced into very tiny pieces

1 pineapple

1 large carrot

salt and pepper to taste

Directions:

Grill chicken breasts until done and set aside to cool. Boil the potatoes (leaving the skin on) until you can pierce them with a fork. Hard boil the eggs and boil the carrot until soft. Put potatoes and eggs in refrigerator to cool down (or they can be cooked in advance by several hours or the day before). Cut the chicken breasts, apples, chilled potatoes and chilled eggs into 1/2-inch cubes and mix ingredients together. Rinse the beans with water until they are unfrozen. Add to the mix. Slice the pickles and cucumbers into 1/2-inch cubes. Mix vegetables together with sour cream, mayonnaise and dill. Salt and pepper to taste.

To serve: Wash a pineapple. Slice lengthwise from the bottom to the top, through to the top of the flower head. Remove the fruit from inside the pineapple using a soupspoon to scoop out rounded pieces. Put the chicken salad inside the pineapple boat and serve.

Serves 4-6

Chicken salad Olivier.

CABBAGE SALAD (JEWISH COLE SLAW)

Ingredients:

1 green cabbage

1/2 red cabbage

Several sprigs of fresh dill

1 apple

1 small carrot

1 tsp fresh lemon juice (squeezed)

1 tbsp olive oil

1/4 tsp sugar

1/2 cup dried cranberries

Directions:

Slice both cabbages. Shred the carrot. Add lemon juice and sugar. Peel and shred the apple. Mix ingredients together. Add olive oil and lightly mix. Cut the dill leaves into small pieces, sprinkle on the top and serve.

Another festive serving option: core 6-8 medium-sized apples and stuff the slaw lightly into the core.

Serves 6-8

CARROT SALAD

Ingredients:

1 lb. carrots

1 tbsp mayonnaise

6 medium green apples

1 tsp squeezed garlic (optional)

Directions:

Shred carrots through the medium-sized slicer holes of the shredder. Add the mayonnaise (and optional garlic). Mix.

To serve: core the center of a medium green apple. Place the carrot mix into the core of each apple.

Alternative: serve without apples as a side dish.

Serves 6 as a substantial salad.

STUFFED POTATOES

Ingredients:

6 baking potatoes or sweet potatoes

1 lb. of cubed meat or chicken

4 tbsp olive oil

salt and pepper to taste

1 egg

2 large yellow onions

Directions:

Cut potatoes in half (not lengthwise). Take a teaspoon and scoop out the potato from its open side but leave about a quarter inch of pulp in the shell.

Make stuffing for the potatoes. Cut meat in cubes and cut 1 onion in cubes. Stir fry the meat and onion together in a pan with about 3 tbls olive oil (enough to fry without burning) until onions are softening and meat is browned. Add salt and pepper to taste.

Grind the fry mix in a food processor or grinder. Add an egg to the mix, as desired.

Take the mix and stuff each potato and place the stuffed potato halves in a glass baking dish. Slice the second onion into half moon rings; fry in pan with a tbsp or so of olive oil until softened. Place onion rings on top of the potatoes. Put water in bottom of baking pan so it reaches almost to the top of the potatoes. Cover baking pan with foil. Bake in oven at 375 for about 20 minutes. Remove foil and bake until potatoes are golden and easily pricked with a fork.

To serve: sprinkle a little chopped dill on top of each potato.

Serves: 12 potato halves (enough for 6 persons as a main course or 12 as a side dish).

CHICKEN BORSCHT

This thick, hearty soup is surprisingly low calorie because it is composed of many different vegetables and skinless chicken. It is a wonderful hot evening dinner.

Ingredients:

2 or 3 pound chicken cut into pieces (6 to 8 pieces) — if you prefer less chicken fat, you can remove the skin

1/2 green cabbage, finely sliced

2 medium sized redskin potatoes, peeled

2 medium or 1 large beet, shredded

2 large cloves of garlic, squeezed

1 large peeled yellow onion

1 large green pepper, cleaned out

1 tsp of salt

1 bunch of parsley, chopped fine (but not the stems)

3 bay leaves

12 oz. tomato paste

Directions:

Fill a large soup pot with 6 quarts of water and bring to a boil. Take a second smaller pot, place chicken pieces in the pot, cover with water, and bring to a boil. When water comes to a boil, empty pot and rinse the chicken. Place the rinsed chicken into the large pot of boiling water and lower water to a simmer. Add the whole onion.

Cook for 40 minutes. From time to time, skim the grease from the top. Cut the pepper into eight pieces and then slice each piece into thin slices. There will be about the same size mound of shredded beets and sliced peppers. Cut the potatoes into 1-inch cubes.

After 40 minutes, remove onion from the pot and add in cut pepper, potatoes, beets, carrots, and tomato paste. Bring to a boil and then turn down to a simmer. Add salt, bay leaves and pepper to taste. In about five minutes, add the cabbage to the pot and cook five minutes. Chop parsley and squeeze the garlic into the pot. Turn off flame, cover pot and move to a cold burner. Let sit in hot pot for 30 minutes.

After sitting, the soup may be served immediately or may be prepared several days in advance, stored in a glass container and reheated for serving.

To serve: ladle soup into bowl and garnish with parsley.

Serves 6-8

Chicken borscht.

DESSERTS

COMPOTE

This dish is rich in vitamins and antioxidants, and a cheerful way to serve dessert during winter.

Ingredients:

1 cup dried apricot

1 cup dried apples

1 cup dried cherries

1 cup dried cranberries

Directions:

Cover the dried fruits with 10 cups of water and bring to a boil. Lower heat and simmer for 5 minutes. Turn off heat and cover pot for 1 hour.

To serve hot: You can drain the liquid or not, according to taste. Spoon the fruit into a bowl; top with a scoop of ice cream; and spoon some of the sauce over the top of the ice cream. You can put drained fruit on top of a latke.

To serve cold: Put the cooked fruit and syrup in the refrigerator and cool. Serve in a fruit dish. You may grate lemon rind over the top. Or serve with a scoop of ice cream. You can pour the liquid into an ice cube tray, freeze and serve in small cups for children to watch melt and drink with a straw.

Serves 6-8

PASSOVER

Matzoh ball soup.

SOUP

MATZOH BALL SOUP

Ingredients:

Buy whole chicken cut into 6-8 pieces

2 yellow onions

1 large carrot or 12 baby carrots

1 bunch of parsley

3 stalks celery

1 lemon/fresh dill/garlic — used to garnish the soup to taste

1 package of matzoh ball mix with the recommended ingredients to make matzoh balls

Directions:

Rinse the chicken pieces. Place pieces in a pot and add enough cold water to just cover the chicken. Bring to a boil and cook for 1 minute. Drain the water and rinse the chicken well.

Fill most of a large pot with clear water and bring to a boil. Then place the chicken in and return it to a boil. The amount of water in the pot should cover the chicken 3 times over. Add the peeled onions and the large carrot (sliced) or whole baby carrots. Once the water is again boiling, lower the heat to a very slow simmer. In 45 minutes, add the parsley and celery. Salt to taste (at least 1/4 tsp). Simmer for 5 minutes. Turn off heat and keep covered for another 30 minutes. Use a slotted spoon to remove all the vegetables except the carrots.

To make the matzoh balls:

Follow package directions — remember to buy those ingredients, also.

After matzoh balls are cooked, heat soup for serving and place balls into hot soup. Serve in a soup tureen or ladled into soup bowls. Garnish with any combination of baby carrot or carrot slice/lemon slice/cut dill/crushed garlic.

Serves 8

Beef tenderloin and vegetables.

MAIN COURSES AND SIDE DISHES

BEEF TENDERLOIN

Ingredients:

1 beef tenderloin (two pounds yields about twelve slices)

2 large garlic cloves cut thin

1 orange or lemon thinly sliced

Salt and pepper

6 bay leaves

Directions:

Cut the tenderloin into 1-inch slices that are cut about 3/4 of the way down through the beef. Slice each garlic clove into thin lengthwise slices. Place a bay leaf between every other slice of beef and place a slice of garlic between the other slices of beef. Lightly salt and pepper the beef. Place beef on tin foil and gently fold the foil over the beef so that the beef is covered but the foil is not touching the top of it.

Cook beef at 400°F. After about 30 minutes open the foil. Cook for another 10 minutes or until the beef is light pink in color. (Because ovens vary in cooking time, we recommend that you check the beef after it cooks for about 40 minute to see its color and check every 10 minutes afterward). Remove beef from oven, take out bay leaves and let sit uncovered for 15 minutes.

Place thin slices of lemon or orange between the meat slices and serve.

Serves 8 to 12

BRISKET

Ingredients:

1 medium to large brisket

1 large yellow onion

12 small Portobello mushrooms

1/4 cup orange juice or pineapple juice

6 sprigs of parsley

6 cloves of garlic

2-3 fresh oranges

salt and pepper

Directions:

Preheat oven to 375. Rub salt and pepper all over the surface of the meat. Slice onions in half moon, enough to cover the bottom of the pan. Pour juice over the top of meat. Place meat in pan. (Glass pan recommended.) Place the cloves of garlic around the meat and place six sprigs of parsley around the meat. Cover meat with tin foil.

Roast meat at 375°F for about 40 minutes. Turn meat over and remove foil and roast for another 25 minutes. If liquid has disappeared from pan, add a little more juice so that meat stays moist. To test if meat is done, cut into meat: the deep inside of the meat should be pink.

While the meat is roasting, prepare the mushrooms. After cleaning the mushrooms, brush lightly with olive oil. Place in a baking dish and bake for 5 to 10 minutes in oven while the meat is roasting. Remove from oven and set aside.

To serve: slice meat at a slight angle. Place slices on a serving platter. Peel fresh oranges and cut each segment in half. Tuck a half segment in between the ends of each piece of meat, so that the segments form a circle around the serving platter alternating with the ends of the meat. Place the mushrooms around the outside of the meat. Place a sprig of fresh parsley on top of every other mushroom.

Note: cold leftover brisket can be served this way or be made into sandwiches.

Serves 6

CHICKEN WITH STEAMED BEER

Ingredients:

2 two-pound chickens

2 small bottles of beer

salt and pepper

2 cloves of garlic, peeled

Directions:

Preheat oven to 375°F. Rinse each chicken and rub the inside and outside with garlic, salt and pepper to taste. Stand end of chicken over the open beer bottom, with chicken's neck facing up. Place chickens with inserted bottle into the oven and bake for 1 hour. Remove chicken and set aside. You may serve the chickens on separate platters with separate accoutrements.

Chicken 1: Serve with mashed potatoes and mushrooms. Spoon mashed potatoes onto the platter in a pile that is about 2 inches thick. Carefully remove the chicken from the bottle and discard beer and bottle. Place the chicken on top of the mashed potatoes. Circle the Portobello mushrooms around the potatoes (see recipe above for baking Portobello mushrooms).

Chicken 2: Serve with stir-fried cabbage (see below for stir fried cabbage recipe). Cover the plate with vegetables, making a pile at least 2 inches high. Shred a fresh carrot over the top of the cabbage. Carefully remove the chicken from bottle, discard beer and bottle, and place chicken on top of the vegetables. Optional: Circle vegetable mix with dried pitted prunes.

Serves 8-12

STIR-FRIED CABBAGE

Ingredients:

2 pounds of green cabbage

2 large yellow onions

2 large Portobello mushrooms

1 tbls dried cranberries

olive oil to use in cooking (up to 1/2 cup)

1 tbls of minced parsley or dill

1 cup of dried pitted prunes (optional)

salt and pepper

Directions:

Slice the onions into half moon slices. Slice mushroom into fine slices. Cut cabbage in half and slice into fine slices. Heat a stir-fry pan/wok with medium heat. (If you don't have a wok, use at least 12-inch frying pan as a substitute). Add olive oil to barely cover pan. Add onions to pan stir and cook for three minutes. Add mushrooms, stir and cook for another 2 minutes. Add cabbage, stir and cook for 3-5 minutes. The cabbage will still be crunchy. Add salt and pepper to taste. Turn off flame and add the cut parsley or dill and dried cranberries and mix together.

BAKED CHICKEN BREASTS

Ingredients:

8 pieces of chicken breast

8 medium (or six large) yellow onions

1 tbls of minced dill

8 medium Portobello mushrooms

1 cup of mayonnaise

salt and pepper

Directions:

Preheat oven to 375. Cut onions into small cubes. Slice the mushrooms. Line the pan with about half the onion cubes (best to use a glass pan). Rub the top and bottom of the breasts with a small amount of salt and pepper. Place the chicken breasts on top of the onions. Cover the breasts with another layer using the other half of the onion cubes.

Place the mushroom slices over the top layer of onions. Using a knife, slather the mayonnaise even over the top of the mushrooms. Cover the pan with aluminum foil. Bake for 30 minutes. Remove foil and bake another 20 minutes. Remove from oven.

To serve: remove each breast from baking dish taking with it the top lawyer of the onions and the mushrooms. Place each breast on a serving platter, making a circle with the pieces. Sprinkle the dill over the top of the pieces and serve.

BAKED WHITEFISH

Ingredients:

1 bunch scallions, chopped

6 tbls horse radish

2 lbs of filleted whitefish — ask store to "butterfly" the fish and remove bones

2 lemons

3 tbls of mayonnaise

1 tbls of squeezed garlic

1 tbls of chopped dill

(Note that this dish is cooked, then chilled and served cold)

Directions:

Preheat oven to 375°F. Rinse fish and pat dry. Squeeze juice from one lemon on both sides of the fillets. Cut the second lemon in half and cut thin half-moon slices from each half. Spread the fish pieces open in a glass baking dish. On top of each open piece put the lemon slices. Spread 1/2 of the chopped scallions on top of the lemon slices. Salt and pepper to taste. Fold over each butterflied fish so that the mix is like the middle of a "sandwich". Salt and pepper again to taste. Spread the remaining scallions on top of the fish. Cover the scallions with mayonnaise. Mix the dill and garlic together and spread on top of the mayonnaise. Cover the dish with aluminum foil being careful not to touch the fish. (You can put two or three toothpicks in the fish to keep the foil away from the fish.) Bake for 40 minutes. When fish is cooked, remove foil. Chill fish in refrigerator for several hours. Serve with horseradish.

MASHED POTATOES

Ingredients:

8 medium baking potatoes

1/8 tsp salt

3 tbls butter

1/2 cup warm milk

Directions:

Peel potatoes, cut in half. Place in pot with water to cover slightly, add 1/8 tsp of salt. Bring water to a boil. Lower heat and gently simmer until potatoes are soft but not mushy (about 20 minutes). Drain water from pot. Add butter and milk. Mash together (with a masher or fork). Serve in serving platter. Optional: sprinkle minced green onions over serving plate. Spoon mashed potatoes into oval-shaped mounds to form a circle around the serving platter. Sprinkle minced dill on top.

Serves 8

BAKED POTATOES

Ingredients:

> 4 medium baking potatoes, evenly sized
>
> 2 tbls butter

Directions:

Rinse potatoes, cut in half lengthwise. With a small spoon, scoop out a small portion of potato from the middle, which will later hold a piece of butter. Rub top of potatoes with a small sprinkling of salt to taste. Place in pan with skin side down. Bake at 375 for about 30 minutes, until you see that the top is gold. You can test doneness with a fork to confirm the potato is soft.

Serving option 1: Garlic and Dill

Ingredients:

> 3 garlic cloves
>
> 2 tbls butter
>
> 2 sprigs of dill

Directions:

Place on serving plate with skin side down. In each middle hole, place a small piece of butter. On top of the butter, squeeze a little garlic and sprinkle minced dill.

Serving option 2: Onion and Mushroom Cover

Ingredients:

> 1 medium yellow onion
>
> 2 Portobello mushrooms

Directions:

Slice onion in half and then the halves into half moon slices. Stir fry with a tablespoon of olive oil. After about 5 minutes, add in sliced mushrooms and stir-fry together for 3 minutes. Remove from pan. Spoon over top of the potatoes.

Serves 8

TSIMMES MOLD

Ingredients:

8 large carrots

4 sweet potatoes

2 tbls dried cranberries

2 tbls yellow raisins

2 tbls dried cherries

2 tbls honey

Vanilla sugar (for taste)

12 pieces dried apricots

1 box Greek yoghurt (or sour cream)

6 tbls roasted almonds, walnuts or pecans

Ground cinnamon

Enough butter or olive oil to grease the
baking dish.

Directions:

Preheat oven to 400°F. Warm a deep, round glass baking dish. Liberally butter or oil the bottom and side of the dish.

Slice the potatoes into two inch slices so that potatoes and carrots are about the same size and shape. Place alternate layers of carrots and potatoes into a glass dish. Sprinkle the dried fruit over each layer before placing the next layer. Add 2 cups of boiling water mixed with two tablespoons of honey. Cover the top with nuts. Bake in oven until carrots and potatoes are soft enough to eat, about 30-40 minutes.

Remove dish from oven and cool enough to handle. Carefully slip tsimmes mold out of dish onto a serving platter.

To serve: Spoon a dollop of Greek yoghurt on top. Sprinkle nuts around the side of the serving plate.

Variation: also drizzle yoghurt around side of the mold. Sprinkle sliced almonds and/or pitted prunes and/or dried apricots around side of mold on top of yoghurt.

Serves 8-12

MATZOH BOBKA (MATZOH BREI)

Ingredients:

1 box matzoh

3 cups of milk

3 medium size Portobello mushrooms

2 large onions

5 eggs

pinch of salt

Enough olive oil to cover pan while cooking
vegetables

Directions:

Tear matzoh in pieces; soak in milk. Peel and cut onions into small cubes; clean and slice mushrooms. Fry onions for about five minutes in olive oil on medium heat, then add sliced mushrooms and continue frying until vegetables are golden. Add the fried mix to the Matzoh. Add mixed eggs, salt and pepper. Heat pan and add olive oil. Add enough mix to the frying pan to cover it for about one inch, then flatten the mix and fry until golden. Flip and fry other side until golden. Add olive oil as needed so that bottom of pan stays greased.

Serve hot or refrigerate and serve cold. Either way, put a dollop of sour cream on top before serving.

Serves 8-12.

Matzoh bobka or brei.

SNACKS

HARD-BOILED EGGS

There are many variations in how to serve tasty hard-boiled eggs and here are some suggestions. These eggs can be served on any Jewish holiday and may be especially appropriate for a Yom Kippur break the fast supper or for Passover meals (breakfast, lunch or dinner). Each recipe is for six people.

To prepare the eggs:

Place cold eggs in pot covered with cold water. Put 1/4 teaspoon salt. Place on stove and bring water to a boil and then lower heat so water is simmering. Cook until hard (typically 7 to 10 minutes of simmering). Empty water and rinse eggs with cold water. Add a few pieces of ice to the cold water so the eggs cool quickly and can be handled. (Alternatively, you can cook the eggs the night before and refrigerate.)

After the eggs are cool enough to handle, peel the shell. Refrigerate until needed. Then, slice each egg lengthwise in half and stuff using one of the recipes below.

EGGS STUFFED WITH MUSHROOMS AND ONIONS

Ingredients:

6 eggs

3 large plum tomatoes

Salt and pepper to taste

1 medium sized yellow onion

1 large Portobello mushroom

Fresh sprigs of parsley

1 tablespoon of Greek yoghurt

Directions:

Slice plum tomatoes in 1/4-inch slices length-wise and set aside. Be sure to save the end slices. Stir fry yellow onions with olive oil until golden and crunchy. Remove yolks from eggs. Mash yolks with fork with salt and pepper to taste. Mix with fried onions and mushrooms. Scoop egg/onion/mushroom mix into egg white halves.

Serve on a flat platter, place tomato slices in a circle around the platter. Place stuffed egg half on top of each tomato slices. On top of stuffed eggs, place a small sprig of parsley or dill. In the middle of the platter, place ends of the sliced tomatoes and on top of them place a dollop of Greek yoghurt.

EGGS WITH CAVIAR AND PARSLEY

Note: caviar is kosher as long as the fish it comes from is kosher. As examples, salmon and whitefish caviar are kosher and you should be able to readily purchase them.

Ingredients:

6 eggs

3 large plum tomatoes

Small jar of red or black caviar

Fresh parsley

6 tablespoons of Greek yoghurt

Salt and pepper to taste

Directions:

Slice plum tomatoes in 1/4-inch slices lengthwise and set aside. Be sure to save the end slices. Boil eggs. Slice eggs in half and remove yolks from eggs. Using a fork, mash yolks with Greek yoghurt and salt and pepper to taste. Stuff the egg whites with the yolk/yoghurt mix.

Serve on a flat platter, place tomato slices in a circle around the platter. Place stuffed egg half on top of each tomato slices. On top of stuffed eggs, place a small dollop or caviar, either red or black or alternating both colors. In the middle of the platter, place a dollop of Greek yoghurt and sprinkle with caviar.

CAVIAR EGG BOATS

Ingredients:

6 hard boiled eggs

12 tablespoons caviar

1 celery stick

1 lemon

6 small round tomatoes (2 inches in diameter)

Directions:

Hard-boil the eggs. Peel, and slice off a sliver of each end so that the egg will sit flat from either end. Cut the egg in half at the middle and scoop out yolks, being careful not to break the egg white. Spoon a tablespoon of red caviar into the inside of each half egg. Slice a thin sliver, about 3 inches long, from the celery stick and poke into the caviar, looking like the handle of a spoon.

Cut each tomato in half and then slice bottom of each half so the tomato half "sits" flat. Scoop out the pulp from each. The tomato quarter will be the "plate" for the caviar egg. Place the egg with caviar and celery plume on top of the tomato. Place on a small plate, garnish with a lemon slice and serve.

Caviar egg boats.

JEWISH STAR SNACK

Ingredients:

1 dozen large matzoh crackers

Cream cheese to spread on crackers

Small jar caviar, red or black

Directions:

Spread cream cheese on cracker. With a knife, shape a Jewish star on the cream cheese and fill with caviar. Ready to serve!

APPLE AND HORSERADISH SNACK

Ingredients:

Dozen large matzoh crackers

1 tbsp of ground horseradish

1/2-inch slices of fresh horseradish

1 large apple, cut in quarters and then into 12 slices.

Directions:

Place small amount of ground horseradish on top of the cracker or a small slice of fresh horseradish. On top of the horseradish, place a slice of apple. For decoration, place a touch of Greek yoghurt or mayonnaise with an almond in the middle.

SMOKED SALMON SNACKS

Ingredients:

12 crackers

12 half moon slices of cucumber

12 half moon slices of lemon

1/2 lb. smoked salmon

1 package of cream cheese

Directions:

Spread cream cheese on each cracker. Place a cucumber and lemon slice on top of each cracker and then a piece of smoked salmon and serve.

Matzoh cake with berries, nuts and jelly fruit slices.
(This picture shows a larger cake made by doubling the recipe.)

DESSERTS

MATZOH CAKE

Ingredients:

- 1 box of unsalted plain matzoh
- 1 lb. of shelled walnuts (pounded into small bits)
- Pinch of vanilla sugar
- 2 cans concentrated milk

- 1 bag of dried cherries or cranberries
- 1 package baker's chocolate
- 1 box fresh blueberries
- 1 package of half moon jellied fruit slices

Directions:

Caramelize milk following these directions: Do not open cans of milk. Place cans in pot, cover with water, bring to boil, reduce heat and simmer for 2-1/2 hours. You can caramelize the milk the day before using, simply set aside, no need to refrigerate.

Use a serving platter large enough to hold a full-sized slice of matzoh with room around the edge for decoration. Place one full slice of matzoh on the platter. Cover the slice with a coat of the caramelized milk and sprinkle the nuts over it. Cover both sides of a second piece of matzoh with the caramelized milk and place that slice on top of the first. Cover the top of the second slice with dried cherries or cranberries. Shred the chocolate on top of the second slice. Place as many layers as you have caramelized milk to cover (maybe 3-4 layers). On the top of the last slice, spread only a little caramelized milk.

You can make the cake the day before up to this point, and decorate the day of serving.

To decorate: You can decorate in lots of ways — see the two pictures as examples. You can sprinkle the top with nuts and dot with whipped cream. Put a blueberry Jewish star on top, or use jelly fruit slices to decorate the edge of the plate and form "butterfly" shapes with a berry "body." Have fun with your imagination!

Matzoh cake with blueberries and strawberries.

CPSIA information can be obtained
at www.ICGtesting.com
Printed in the USA
BVHW011535100321
602204BV00010B/365